A FAITH FOUNDATION TO FINANCIAL FREEDOM

Boldly Choose Success

by Stafford B. Sutton, Jr.

Printed in the United States of America, 2005.

ISBN: 0-9749223-1-5

Credits
Consulting and editing   Cover and page design   Production Services
On-time Writing   Kouba Graphics, Inc.   Evans Graphics Consultants

A FAITH FOUNDATION TO FINANCIAL FREEDOM

Boldly Choose Success

STAFFORD B. SUTTON, JR.

SES CHURCH FINANCIAL

A FAITH FOUNDATION TO FINANCIAL FREEDOM
Boldly Choose Success

DEDICATION

The words "thank you" seem insufficient to describe the depth of my gratitude to my family for their unwavering support of all my endeavors. I thank my family for being encouraging as I have traveled this journey—Hattie Sutton; Brandon Sutton; Stafford Sutton, Sr.; Bertha Sutton; Ted Sutton and Chris Sutton.

It is not an easy task to share your innermost personal experiences with the world. I want people to understand what I have experienced on my journey to financial fitness so that the lessons I have learned can help someone else. Knowledge of the tools necessary to achieve financial independence can make all the difference in structuring your individual financial fitness plan. So I also dedicate this book to those who read it. My sincere prayer is that it will serve as a useful tool in your individual commitment to achieve and strengthen your financial independence.

A Faith Foundation to Financial Freedom

INTRODUCTION

Have you ever felt like a total failure, like you're facing the world all alone? Have you known what it's like to think that you've let yourself down and let down your friends and family? Have you hit rock bottom and just felt too embarrassed to face the truth?

If you have, then we have something in common. I've been there, done that and felt just that way. I was a successful young entrepreneur, buying and restoring properties. I made a fortune before I was 25 years old. Then I lost my fortune practically overnight.

I was in business with a partner who betrayed my trust. But my deeper trust has always been in God. So I gave my troubles to Him and I went back to work rebuilding my finances. I am grateful that I faced that loss when I was young enough to recover. I learned to trust again but to be more careful. Financially and personally, I regained my perspective and optimism. My partner may have turned out to be untrue, but God's grace and greatness was steadfast. He had other things in store for me.

My experience from all those years ago taught me the real value of what I have—the life and health I've been given, my reputation, the talents I've been blessed with and the freedom I enjoy to decide and create my own life's course. I never forget who I am as a person, what I mean to my family and friends and what they mean to me.

I know that your finances don't define you. I am proud of who I was then and who I am today and I know that helps me define who I'll be tomorrow. I believe we have to approach life with an attitude of stewardship. Life, freedom, family—all are very valuable gifts. We have choices in how we appreciate and manage everything that God gives us. How we use God's blessings reflects our thankfulness.

I am here as a testimony that faith can help you find financial freedom and live a more fulfilling life. God has the power to help you take control, even if you're starting from that rock-bottom place. I'm now convinced that God led me through my financial troubles so I can help others seek His help in the financial part of their lives. Finding our true purpose in Him is a blessing and joy like no other.

—Stafford B. Sutton, Jr.

A Faith Foundation to Financial Freedom

PART 1

YOUR MONEY MANAGEMENT PERSONALITY

I can do all things

through Christ

which strengteneth me.

— Philippians 4:13

NOTES

PART 1

YOUR MONEY MANAGEMENT PERSONALITY

----------- ☙❧ -----------

The Apostle Paul said in Philippians 4:13, "I can do all things through Christ which strengtheneth me." As Christians, we should be buoyed by this statement of faith and optimism.

Why is it, then, that so many Christians are bound by depression, negativity and hopelessness when it comes to financial matters? If we can indeed do all things—and with Christ's help, we can—why is it so difficult to get a handle on money matters, when they are such a big part of our lives?

There is a better way. A faith-based approach to financial freedom can lead you to a more productive, purposeful life.

But first you have to start by recognizing the deep-seated attitudes that you have toward money matters. Generally, I've found four basic profiles in relationship to money management: Extravagant, Realistic, Calculated and Emotional. Most of us have pieces of all the characters in us and these examples take the differences to the extreme. You can examine yourself in the light of these character types and evaluate where you can adjust. In fact, at the end of this section, you'll be doing just that.

NOTES

A Faith Foundation to Financial Freedom

THE EXTRAVAGANT MONEY MANAGER

Let's call the extravagant personality Bob. Everyone knows a Bob. He is a "get it now" person. He wants to be the first to have the latest gadget, newest car or trendiest clothing. He calls the ATM the "money machine" and he treats it like that's exactly what it is. He can't tell you his bank balance and wouldn't think of balancing his checkbook. (I've actually known some people of this type who would call the bank every month or two to see what their balances were. They never kept track!)

Bob indulges himself. His attitude is, "I want it. I deserve it. I'll get it." He's big into immediate gratification. Bob can be generous when it's all for show, like picking up the tab or leaving a big tip.

Bob also is inclined to indulge his family. He buys his wife diamonds at Christmas although she'd rather have more of his time. He thinks his kids should have the best, too, and often gives in to their pleas for expensive shoes, prom dresses and things they like. "So what if I can't afford it?" says Bob. "I really love my kids!"

Bob rarely pays *for* anything; he's paying *on* everything. He makes the minimum payments on his credit accounts. When Bob finds he's maxing out his credit cards, he starts looking for a deal on a new one that will accept roll-overs from his exhausted cards. He may be drowning in debt but it isn't changing his lifestyle. He's carefree.

Bob defines his self-worth through spending. Saving is not in his vocabulary. His motto is "You can't take it with you." He's always waiting to win the lottery or hit the jackpot, but if he did, he'd blow right through his winnings.

Oh, Bob's had to face his spending habits in the past. In fact, he cuts up all his credit cards about once a decade, but before you know it, he's right back where he started. Spending is Bob's addiction and he has never been able to control it for long.

A Faith Foundation to Financial Freedom

THE REALISTIC MONEY MANAGER

Mary is realistic about her money. She's thoughtful about her purchases and is sure to get her money's worth. For big expenditures, she does her homework, checks consumer reports and watches for sales. She usually pays all her credit cards in full at the end of each month. Well, there was that time when she needed the new dining room furniture before the whole family came for Thanksgiving, but she promised herself she'd have it paid off in four months, and she kept that promise.

Mary isn't interested in flaunting her money. She's content with a comfortable lifestyle, nothing too fancy or showy. She drives an economical sedan and likes the fact that it was paid for in three years. She'll buy a new car every five or six years.

Mary has a nice, little emergency savings account—in case something goes wrong with that paid-off car and she needs repairs. But she's also putting away some money in her IRA at work and has a mutual fund. She saved up for the down payment on her home and she makes an extra payment when she can manage to, so she can pay the mortgage off quicker and save all that interest she deplores.

Mary uses a debit card and she records every deduction and check she writes. She doesn't have to wait for the bank statement because she knows what's in her account.

Mary's realistic. She knows money is the means, not the end, but she wants her money to work for her and has a good comfort level with her balance of saving and spending. She feels she has something to show for her money.

Mary started a small savings account for each of her children when they were born. She puts a little in them every month and is watching them grow slowly. She doesn't give in to every spending whim of her children. In fact, she tries to teach them about money by giving them an allowance and helping them weigh their spending options.

THE CALCULATED MONEY MANAGER

Paul balances his checkbook to the penny. In fact, he uses a computer program so he can sort his expenses and print out different reports. Paul may have any occupation, but he's got accounting in his blood. Paul uses the ATM so rarely he has to think hard to remember his PIN. He gets a set amount of spending cash at each pay check and makes it last.

Paul saves and pays cash for almost every purchase, including his cars, which he never buys brand-new because they devalue so quickly. He likes to find the best deal for every purchase he makes. He has to plan well in advance before buying, but he doesn't mind. Paul carries no credit balances and he even makes sure he gets rewards for using a credit card. If it weren't for those perks and the fact that the credit statement makes it so easy to account for his expenses, he probably wouldn't use credit cards at all.

Paul is on his way to becoming one of those "millionaires next door." No one can tell by his lifestyle that he has plenty of money in the bank and in his investment portfolio. He lives simply, drives an old car because he's maintained it well and defines his self-worth through what he's managed to stash away. He takes his lunch to work and takes his wife out to dinner only on special occasions. He thinks it's much better—and cheaper—to eat at home.

To make sure his family is taken care of, Paul has built an estate plan. He'll leave a sum to charity in his will, too, but you can be sure it will go to an organization he's checked out thoroughly or is deeply involved with. (Maybe he's been its volunteer treasurer!)

Paul likes useful things and is sometimes confused by his kids' demands for big-label clothes or luxuries, when the ordinary options are just as functional. He's concerned more about making his kids' future secure than in seeing that they keep up with their friends' latest fads. He figures they may not appreciate his perspective now, but they'll understand later.

Paul's watchword is, "It's not what you make; it's what you save that counts."

THE EMOTIONAL MONEY MANAGER

Emotional money managers have big hearts. They've never had much of a head for finances and still manage to get by over the years. They may or may not balance their checkbook. They will make cash withdrawals and then be surprised by their balance.

Take Sue, for example. Sue is very helpful and feels responsible for everyone else's happiness. Consequently, when her nephew calls and needs a loan because his car has broken down, she will give him the money even if she doesn't really have it to give. She will deny herself little necessities to indulge her granddaughter. She knows she can't afford to do these things but she has this mentality of always rescuing others.

Unfortunately, Sue stretches her money with her credit cards. It's been years since she had a zero balance on any of them. She's sick with worry about it but can't seem to make any progress toward getting out of debt. About the time she resolves to "just say no" to one of her family members, she gets another SOS call and once again sacrifices her own financial well-being to help them out.

Sue gives until it hurts, literally, but if confronted, she'd say, "But what good is money if you can can't help others with it?" Deep down she wonders if she's just trying to buy their love. Sue's children never learned the value of money. She spoiled them and continues to be their safety net. In a way, Sue is happy to be so needed.

Sue's generosity with her church and charities is laudable. She believes she will be rewarded for her giving spirit, but if her pastor or others knew what she sometimes sacrifices in order to give, they might offer to help her instead. She pretends she has no financial stresses and she really is pleased by the attention her gifts bring her.

Sue never learned the wisdom of "paying yourself first." She has not put aside much for her future. She spends now and figures the future will take care of itself. She knows there will probably be consequences but she just doesn't want to think about it and she feels helpless to control it anyway.

A Faith Foundation to Financial Freedom

YOUR MONEY MANAGEMENT PERSONALITY

Now for your own profile. On the next page, you'll find a chart with the four money management profiles and brief descriptions. Following that is a blank chart. Beside each spending behavior, put a check mark in the box under Extravagant, Realistic, Calculated or Emotional to indicate where you think your spending habits fall. Chances are, you'll be a mix of the different characteristics. That's OK. This chart will help you to see yourself more clearly, and that's a big step in the right direction if you want to change how you manage money and achieve financial fitness.

I believe the best way to make lasting change is to lay the foundation in your faith. God wants his children to be the best that they can be. He has a special purpose for each of us. As you examine how you're spending your life and your money, I hope that you will feel God leading you to make better decisions in everything you do. Your willingness to change and God's grace can make it possible for you to achieve financial fitness.

Remember, we all make choices and we can make better choices at any time. It's never too late to make improvements and learn new ways to achieve your goals. The remainder of this book will walk you through steps so, with faith as the foundation of your financial matters, you can BOLDLY CHOOSE SUCCESS.

MONEY MANAGEMENT PERSONALITY TYPES

	Extravagant	Realistic	Calculated	Emotional
Spending Journey				
Bank Account Status	Doesn't know account balance and does not balance checkbook. Spends no matter what.	Knows balance of account but not the details. Spends, but does not go over.	Balances checkbook to the penny.	May or may not balance checkbook. Spends as needed.
Purchase Habits	Pays "on it" not "for it."	Pays for it.	Saved to be able to pay for it.	May deny themselves in order to buy for others.
ATM/Debit Usage	Depends on the ATM. It's a money machine.	Uses debit card but does not take out cash.	Rarely uses ATM. Knows the usage fees. Schedules ATM withdrawals.	Withdraws cash as needed and is surprised by balance.
Spending Justification	I want it. I deserve it. I'll buy it now.	Thoughtful about purchases. Buys within reason.	Plans spending for the future. Plans before purchasing.	Buys now and addresses consequences later.
Credit Status	Drowning in debt but carefree. Looking to obtain more credit cards.	In control of credit. Doesn't let balances hang over them for long.	Carries no credit balances. Obtains rewards for credit spending.	Stretched to the limit financially, and often sick with worry, but unable to take control.
Money Motivation	Waiting to win the lottery or hit the jackpot.	Obtaining a comfortable lifestyle.	Becoming the millionaire next door.	Sharing even when they can't afford to.
Comfort Level Comes From	Self indulgence, the now mentality.	Things they have from what they invested.	What they have saved.	A "savior" mentality, always rescuing others.
Self Worth Defined	Through spending.	Through a balance of saving and spending.	Through saving.	Through giving.
Slogan	You can't take it with you.	Money is the means, not the end.	It's not what you make, it's what you save.	What good is money if you can't help others with it?

A Faith Foundation to Financial Freedom

My Personal Money Management Profile

	Extravagant	Realistic	Calculated	Emotional
Spending Journey				
Bank Account Status				
Purchase Habits				
ATM Usage				
Spending Justification				
Credit Status				
Money Motivation				
Comfort Level Comes From				
Self Worth Defined				
Slogan				

NOTES

A Faith Foundation to Financial Freedom

PART 2

FAITH'S FOUNDATION

Abide in me, and I in you.

As the branch cannot bear fruit of itself,

except it abide in the vine;

no more can ye, except ye abide in me.

I am the vine, ye are the branches;

He that abideth in me, and I in him,

the same bringeth forth much fruit:

for without me, ye can do nothing.

— John 15:4-5

NOTES

PART 2

FAITH'S FOUNDATION

—————————— ⋯ ——————————

You may think if you don't have much money, your approach to financial matters doesn't make much difference. Even when you have only a little, how you use what you have can shape your future. But if you're not faithful in managing the little you have, you won't be faithful with much more. The same holds true with management of your time and talent as well as resources. All these things are valuable assets you need to succeed in life. With your faith as a foundation, you can make the best use of God's blessings and lead a fruitful life, free of financial stresses.

Before we start this discussion, I want to make it clear that I know—and I hope you know—that money won't buy happiness. No amount of worldly goods can bring you peace of mind. Riches cannot wipe shame and sin from your heart, only God's grace can do that. What I advocate is using your faith and some good common sense to practice smart, spiritual stewardship of whatever material things you have. That good stewardship can be rewarding for you personally and it can enable you to be in a position to help your family and others. I hope you agree that, after providing security for your family, the best part of having material things is being able to share with others close to your heart and reinvest in your community.

An important part of our faith walk is to recognize the critical role God plays in our purpose, our financial journey and security. The Bible tells us that God does not change. If God does not change and he wants us to have the desires of our heart, then we must stop and question the choices that affect our journey. Who must change? The change must occur within us. How often have we seen financial miracles? I saw a single mother with three children win a brand new car. What a miracle that happened to her on her journey, yet those miracles do not always happen to others. The lesson in life is simply that God allows experiences to occur in our lives to move us closer to our purpose. We must believe our problems can be resolved. We must walk the journey of faith and trust and learn from each bump along the way.

Fulfilling your purpose
gives inspiration to
others to fulfill theirs.

I've known very successful people who made millions. A businessman named Peter, who attended our financial seminar, shared an unbelievable testimony. He owned numerous homes, cars, designer suits—every need and want was met. When his business failed, he did not understand why it happened. He did not practice smart, faithful stewardship. The money was gone and he was no longer able to help his family, friends or church. He felt God had changed. Why was God allowing this to happen to him? He still wanted a fancy lifestyle and was angry.

God is always the same. So we must believe this business-man's life change happened for a purpose. Maybe God was using this situation to restore his faith foundation. This was an area where he had to stretch. Our journey to financial fitness may lead us down a difficult winding path of life. For many people, their true God-given purpose may escape them altogether. During the journey, Peter might look at his situation and increase his faith or get frustrated. It's a decision only he can make. How are you walking your faith journey? Are you looking at the miracles of others or learn-ing from the lessons that occur in your life each day?

We need to believe that miracles can happen and we need to believe that everything happens to us for a reason. God gives us purpose and he gives us events to stretch us, to help us grow outside our comfort zone. As we walk on our journey, others can be inspired through our lives and testi-mony. Fulfilling your purpose gives inspiration to others to fulfill theirs.

NOTES

A Faith Foundation to Financial Freedom

ℬ

BELIEVE THAT GOD'S WORD IS TRUE.

For unto whomsoever much is given,

of him shall be much required;

and to whom men have committed much,

of him they will ask the more.

— Luke 12:48

NOTES

B

BELIEVE THAT GOD'S WORD IS TRUE.

One of my favorite New Testament parables is found in Matthew 25:14-30. You're probably familiar with the story of the talents, about a man who gave five talents, two talents and one talent to each of three servants before he left on a trip. A talent was equivalent to a sizable sum of money and the story says the man gave to each servant according to that servant's ability, so he had an idea of what they were capable of achieving.

When the man returned, he learned the servant who had been given five talents earned five more. The servant given two talents also had doubled what was entrusted to him. The third servant, however, was fearful and simply hid his one talent and had only that to return to the master. The first two servants were rewarded with the guardianship of many things because they had been faithful with a few, but the third servant was cast out.

There are lots of things to think about in this parable—as there are, no doubt, in all parables! You could say it means we should not just "sit on" the gifts we've been given but should put them to use, whether they are large or small.

You might say it endorses risk-taking or overcoming our fears. Does it mean if you take a leap of faith, it will always be rewarded?

What if one of the servants had risked his trust but lost it? "Master, I invested in sheep but the price of mutton fell while you were gone." Would that course have been better than simply hiding his trust?

Whatever messages you may take from this parable, I think we can agree that God intends for His people to be good stewards of what they have. We accept a certain responsibility to treat money as a blessing from God and we have an obligation for stewardship of that blessing, however large or small it may be.

Examine how you invest your life. Take the time to discover yourself and find your talents.

It's wasteful to do nothing with your time, talents or God's tithe. All are interest-bearing valuables. Examine how you invest your life. Take the time to discover yourself and find your talents. Just as your tenth belongs to God and is spiritual and is required for a blessing, so your other parts of life should be subject to God and viewed as a blessing. View whatever you've been given by God as an investment. Take what you have and trust God to use it and multiply it through your faith. Make good, informed choices in everything you do.

Handling your finances well should be a reflection of your faith. Do you trust God in everything but your finances? Why would you leave God out of that important part of your life? Believe that God's word is true and trust Him in everything.

NOTES

OPEN YOUR HEART, MIND AND SPIRIT TO WHAT GOD HAS IN STORE FOR YOU.

You did not choose me,

but I chose you and appointed you

that you should go and bear fruit,

and that your fruit should remain,

that whatever you ask the Father

in my name

He may give you.

— John 15:16

NOTES

A Faith Foundation to Financial Freedom

OPEN YOUR HEART, MIND AND SPIRIT TO WHAT GOD HAS IN STORE FOR YOU.

———————— ⋘⋙ ————————

How do you start on the path to financial stability if you don't know where you're going? I believe you must spend some time discovering God's purpose for your life. You must do some soul-searching to discover your gifts and talents. Don't let your life's essence slip away. Your purpose will propel you to prosperity. If you feel in your heart you're doing what you're supposed to do, you'll find life is happier and things seem to flow easier.

> ***Don't let your life's essence slip away.***
> ***Your purpose will propel***
> ***you to prosperity.***

Of course, not everyone has the same purpose or talents. That is part of the wonderful diversity God created in us. Each of us is an individual and we each have our own purpose. Don't question someone else's gifts or your own. Don't ask, "Why didn't I get that talent?" Enjoy and be thankful for your gifts, for all gifts are important in God's sight. Just like different parts of the body help us function as a whole being, so God's plan requires different people with different gifts, but all are needed for His purpose.

Maybe it's someone's purpose to become a great neurosurgeon. Maybe it's someone else's to be the parent that nurtures the interests in a child who grows up to be that neurosurgeon. It may be one person's purpose to preach the Gospel; it maybe another's to be a witness every day in a retail job, encountering all kinds of customers who need to hear a cheerful voice that restores hope. One purpose is not less than another. They are just different.

Do some soul searching. Sit down and write two columns listing your strengths and things you need to work on. What do you bring to the table as a person? Maybe you're a born promoter, a team-builder, a leader or a dedicated behind-the-scenes worker. Examine your interactions with family, friends and coworkers. How is the group better because of you and the personal resources you bring to the table?

Think about the contributions you make (or should be making) to the church, the community or a volunteer organization. What activities are important to you? Are you spending your time and money building relationships that strengthen your values, your worth and your identity? Evaluate your emotional investments. How can you improve your commitment to God, your family or your significant other?

Assessing your values—really doing some personal analysis—will help you discover how your faith can shape your financial future. What is important to you? Take stock of your values and understand how you think and why you manage your life and money the way you do. Look at the big picture, your dreams and plans for the future. God has great things in store for us. But we must put ourselves in His hands and be open to all the wondrous possibilities.

NOTES

A Faith Foundation to Financial Freedom

LEARN FROM OTHERS.

Ask, and it shall be given you;

seek, and ye shall find;

knock, and it shall be opened unto you:

For every one that asketh receiveth;

and he that seeketh findeth;

and to him that knocketh

it shall be opened.

—Matthew 7:7-8

NOTES

Learn from others.

Have your experiences been preparing you for your purpose? If you can determine the things you are passionate about and map your life connected to that passion, the passion gives your life purpose as you use your talents daily. If you know where your talents lie, then you need a plan to get where you want to go so you can use those talents to the fullest. You need to get directions.

Before you head off somewhere in your car, you get directions, right? You ask someone you know or you consult a source you trust and map out where you're going. If you get lost along the way, you can stop and ask directions before you drive on. You don't necessarily have to know the person; strangers are usually willing to give directions. The same thing applies to your search for purpose and a path for life.

Start with the people you know and who know you best. Talk with parents, relatives, teachers, friends and others acquainted with you. Ask questions to find out what they perceive as your greatest talents. Confide what you think may be the purpose you're called for and get reactions.

Then don't be afraid to reach out and contact people who are already successful in doing the kinds of things you feel led to do. Like when you're lost and ask directions, you need to find someone who knows the territory, who has taken that path, and who can speak to you as an expert in that field. Teacher, salesperson, therapist, artist, carpenter, interior designer, chef—whatever your think your calling is, you can find someone who is willing to talk to you about their vocation. Seek counsel of a pastor if you're considering the ministry. Contact a nurse or physician if you're thinking of a medical career. Talk to people who own their own businesses if you think you're an entrepreneur. Ask your sources: How did you get started? Why did you choose this field? What does it take in terms of time and education to do what you do?

Don't be afraid to reach out and contact people who are already successful in doing the kinds of things you feel led to do.

Learn from the responses you get both from the people who know you and experts you contact. Be accepting of direction and positive criticism. At first you may feel vulnerable, but if you make an effort it usually will be rewarded with some sound advice to help you on your way. The whole experience will stretch you outside your comfort zone and challenge you to move farther in your expectations of yourself and your possibilities.

Whether you have to seek counsel or enroll in some institution to learn more, your personal growth is among the best investments you can make. You'll gain confidence, which is so valuable in the marketplace, and knowledge, so you'll know what you're talking about and can be a problem-solver. These things are important because others want confident, knowledgeable people on their teams, regardless of what they do.

Getting an education through working on a degree or certification may not always mean you know so much more than the next person, but it says you have exercised the discipline required to complete the work and obtain the recognition. It speaks to your ability to handle deadlines and pressures, to complete projects on time and to interact with others who are learning.

It's true, we don't all excel at the same things and it may be impractical to think you can be a physician if the sight of blood makes you faint. Just remember God has given us all talents and we can grow spiritually by using those talents. Focus on what you do well naturally and you will find your purpose there. Once you're sure of your direction, beware of naysayers, people who want to put a damper on your dreams and aspirations. Be willing to seek answers and to adopt the spirit of a humble learner so God can use you and your individual purpose.

NOTES

A Faith Foundation to Financial Freedom

DETERMINE YOUR DESTINY.

For God has not given us a spirit of fear,
but of power and of love and of a sound mind.
Be not thou therefore ashamed
of the testimony of our Lord,
but be thou partaker of the afflictions
of the Gospel according to the power of God;
Who hath saved us, and called us with
an Holy Calling, not according to our works,
but according to His own purpose and grace,
which was given us in Christ Jesus
before the world began.
— II Timothy 1:7-9

NOTES

A Faith Foundation to Financial Freedom

Determine your destiny.

I don't believe in half-hearted success. We become great when our commitment to our goal is great. Whatever you want to do with your life, the commitment may be costly. Ask yourself if you're willing to pay the price to obtain success. Are you willing to go back to school, work two jobs or take a low-paying position to get your foot in the door?

For a while, I actually worked for nothing so I could learn about the field I knew I was suited for. My father was a pastor, so I grew up in the ministry. I had some understanding of how churches worked. I believed I could help churches with financial success. I began to learn the church finance industry, to see how banks and mortgage companies related to church needs. I had the opportunity to work with small clients and eventually was paid a little monthly stipend. I specialized in numbers and issues related to church work. God had prepared me and all this laid the foundation for eventually starting my own company. Securing millions of dollars for ministry is connected to my purpose.

Many people fail to realize their purpose or greatness because no one proclaims it to them and they don't claim it for themselves. There is as much greatness in a fulfilled life as a clerk as there is in that of a Nobel Prize winner. We might measure them differently, but God's measure is the same. Each must do the best with what he has. God gives each of us purpose and our measure of greatness is fulfilling that purpose, whatever it is.

Think about David. He was already great as a shepherd when the prophet Samuel came to anoint him and proclaim his great purpose as the future king. He needed to step out and walk into his destiny. To slay a bear was great; to slay a lion was great. Both of these animals would have killed the sheep he attended. God was his strength. It was only through God that he slew those dangerous animals. David had not yet realized who he was to the world—the great future king of Israel—but he did know that he was special to God.

We become great when our commitment to our goal is great.

He was special to God because he would humble himself and praise God. He would admit when he had failed and give God the glory when he triumphed over his enemies. He was a man after God's own heart. God was with him when the odds against him seemed almost impossible. And we should take a lesson from that: We are all special to God.

We are his children, and He will be with us through challenges we think are impossible.

According to the story in I Samuel, no one expected David to be able to conquer the Philistine Goliath, but he was prepared when the challenge arose. He showed bravery and stood up to one of his greatest tests. And afterward, scripture says, "David behaved himself wisely." He may not have looked the role of a leader but that's what he became.

You don't need a Samuel to come and proclaim your greatness and your purpose. I believe we all have it in us—a kind of holy DNA—that binds us to God and the purpose He has for our lives. We can treat that as a dominant gene or recessive gene. We let it be our foundation or we can ignore its influence. You can seize opportunities to determine where you want your life to go, or you can drift along aimlessly if you are not fully in tune with God's purpose for your life.

We each are given one lifetime to fulfill our purpose. We must claim it and live fully so in the end we have poured out our purpose in all we have done. Proverbs 23:7 tells us, "As [a man] thinketh in his heart, so is he." If you've been on the wrong path, there is time to change your way of thinking. If you've been stifled and bound by abuse or neglect or something else in your past, pray and work to get past it. Sometimes such tragedies that happen to us have a reason, to help us become a witness and help others. Let God use your unique experiences to reach out and touch others in ways that someone without your experiences cannot. You may be able to relate to someone God is trying to reach.

Get over the excuses and the pity party and take up your purpose. *Declare yourself no longer a victim but a victor.* Then move forward. Your past choices do not dictate your future choices. You can change directions from your past. Make a different choice and make a difference in your life. Every day commit spiritually to your purpose. Remember you can grow through adversity and come out stronger because of it. Repeat Rev. Jesse Jackson's chant, "I am somebody!" Allow your attitude to help determine your altitude.

LIVE YOUR PASSION.

Whatsoever thy hand findeth to do,

do it with thy might;

for there is no work, nor device,

nor knowledge, nor wisdom,

in the grave, whither thou goest.

— Ecclesiastes 9:10

NOTES

A Faith Foundation to Financial Freedom

LIVE YOUR PASSION.

Whatever your hands find to do, says the scripture, do it with your might. I think that means live with passion. When you've invested the time to discover God's purpose for your life, you can pursue it with passion, putting aside doubts and fears. If you're called to be a teacher, be the best teacher you can be. If you're called to be a repairman, be the best and most honest repairman in town. How you do your job is more important than the type of job you do.

You may get job satisfaction from helping your fellowman. Laboring in the service of others may be your passion. That's important. You may reach someone through your service. We are our brothers' keepers. The way you live your life is an example to the people you meet on the job everyday, whether they are part of your work team or the clients you help. They should be able to see Christ in your life, whatever you do. Your example every day of your life could be a testimony for Christ, whether you're a garbage collector, a postal carrier, a receptionist, a hairdresser or an insurance agent. If you're working in tune with your purpose, you will live with passion, joy and energy that are contagious. You can't help but radiate God's spirit.

A man in my Sunday School class said that when he was a young man, he struggled for two years trying to determine whether God was leading him into the ministry. Then circumstances and prayer led him to believe that God was leading him not to be in the ministry but to be a good community and church leader, an example for other laymen of a godly man outside the ministry. And he has been true to that calling for more than 30 years. He is not in the ministry, but he lives his life with a passion and for God. His life influences others.

For some people, finding their passion means coming to rely on themselves for their livelihood. This is a path I took. Following your passion and becoming an entrepreneur is a big step of faith. Owning your own business is only one way to pursue your passion, but it represents fulfillment to me. Building a legacy and inheritance for my family is rewarding, but I have found that working for myself takes discipline as well as commitment.

Anyone who wants to start a business must ask themselves if they are willing to accept the challenges required of an entrepreneur. You can choose to use your talents to the fullest and realize all that God has planned for you to be or you can choose to let your life's essence slip away. Your choice can affect your family, employees and other people who love you. But the effects are multiplied when you are an entrepreneur.

Since owning my own business, I've come to terms with the fear of failure. As a business owner, I have to be concerned about employees as well as family. They're counting on the continued growth and success of my company for their own financial future. So I feel a big sense of personal responsibility to all of them not to fail. I constantly pray and encourage myself to remember that God has already given me the talent, passion and determination to succeed. My company will continue to prosper as I walk in the confidence of God's purpose for my life. I trust Him to give me wisdom to make good decisions in both my professional and personal life.

Living your passion puts you in sync with your God-given talents and your purpose in life.

Last year a local news program carried a story about a hospital administrator who was laid off during the economic downturn a couple of years ago. Already in his late 40s, he wasn't having a very promising job search, even though he'd been very good at his job. With time on his hands, he began researching the Web and reading books about working with copper. Before long, he set up a shop in his garage and began to hand-tool copper lamp shades with Western, African, nature and patriotic themes. He uses readily available mesquite wood for bases, but finely turns and polishes them into works of art. Some of his creations command up to $1,000 each.

The reporter asked, "If the hospital came knocking and offered you your old job back, what would you say?" The lamp maker replied, "They already have and I turned them down."

Isn't that amazing? He had to lose his job to find his passion but now he is pursuing it and there's no turning back. He's more fulfilled in his life than ever before. That tells you God had a purpose in mind all along, doesn't it?

You may have an artistic flair and can find success as an artist, interior designer or some other creative career. Maybe you love reading and writing and could find fulfillment working for a literacy program. Perhaps you could turn a talent for something physical like skateboarding into a retail franchise or a practice arena. Maybe you have the gifts to be a personal trainer, a real estate broker or public speaker. You can practice your passion working in a large company or a small one or working for yourself.

Start to make a list of things you like to do, talents that you were born with or have learned, interests you've acquired or things you know how to teach. Do your day job with all the passion it deserves and pursue other passions through volunteering or part-time jobs. Who knows? Perhaps what you've done as a hobby may eventually become a full-time job and lead you into new things.

There are thousands of ways to live your passion. I can personally testify that living your passion puts you in sync with your God-given talents and your purpose in life.

You hold your future in your hands.

This book of the law
shall not depart out of thy mouth;
but thou shalt meditate therein day
and night, that thou mayest observe to do
according to all that is written therein:
for then thou shalt make thy way prosperous,
and then thou shalt have good success.
— Joshua 1:8

NOTES

A Faith Foundation to Financial Freedom

You hold your future in your hands.

◄►

It's up to you to make investments in yourself that create a positive future. We each have choices to make in life; whether to be happy, fulfilled, honest or anything else is your own choice. Regardless of where you stand today—young, old, rich, poor—you have the choice to make the most of what you have been given.

> *Is your faith big enough to overcome your fear of not succeeding?*

We may not start with the same advantages, but we have the capacity to use our God-given abilities to accomplish great things. And, unfortunately, we also have the capacity to waste great fortunes and advantages if we make poor choices. Learning to manage what you have means you value yourself enough to build your life and take control of your future, including your finances. Every day you make financial decisions that can affect your life in the long term, not just here and now. Making the best decisions is often a matter of where you put your faith. Is your faith big enough to overcome your fear of not succeeding?

If you build your life around God, it will be good. Having a relationship with God, daily communing and talking with Him will ensure your life is in His will. Our Father wants only the best for us. Israel was God's chosen nation, blessed from the beginning, and their experiences made them stronger, yet the Israelites were capable of destroying their own blessing when they turned from their faith. We as Christian believers can also stand in the way of our own blessing. We can choose to ignore God and not walk with Him and let Him lead us or we can commune in the Holy Spirit and let Him lead us to our destiny.

God values every individual, why should we not value ourselves and commit to having better lives? If you believe God's word is true, open your heart to what He has in store for you, learn from others, determine your destiny and live your passion, you will be able to use your life as a tool to live well and inspire others. This foundation of faith—your confidence in God and in your own value in His sight—will prepare you for a future free of financial encumbrances, free to fulfill your true purpose.

For the next 30 days, after you finish this book, take the time to journal what you have learned and what you can do differently to move toward your purpose. It's my prayer that you understand the connections between what God has given you and your responsibility to use all his blessings wisely. Your future is in your hands.

CHECK YOUR VALUES IDENTITY

I. What do I want to accomplish in the next year, five years, 10 years?

Next year:_____

Five years: _____

Ten years: _____

II. What are my dreams?

_____

III. What can I do now to help me reach these goals?

_____

IV. My three strongest traits are:

1. _____

2. _____

3. _____

V. Three things I need to work on are:

1. _____

2. _____

3 _____

VI. If I died tomorrow, people who know me would remember me as:

_____

VII. The top five things I really value in life are:

1. _____

2. _____

3. _____

4. _____

5. _____

VIII. Does how you spend your time and money reflect your values?

How? _____

Why or why not? _____

NOTES

Part 3

Financial Freedom

The steps of a good man

are ordered by the Lord:

and he delighteth in his way.

Though he fall,

he shall not be utterly cast down:

for the Lord upholdeth him with His hand.

I have been young and now am old;

yet have I not seen the righteous forsaken,

nor his seed begging bread.

— Psalms 37:23-25

NOTES

A Faith Foundation to Financial Freedom

PART 3

FINANCIAL FREEDOM

So what does all this talk about money management personalities and God's purpose for your life have to do with your financial choices?

How you're perceived in this world hinges on your values, including your financial values. How people look upon your character has much to do with your trustworthiness and the confidence they place in your words and ideas. Bankers, employers, landlords, and even insurance companies make judgments about your values based on your financial situation. And they are not the only people who may view your character through your credit history.

Good people want to interact with others who make smart choices and have integrity. Coworkers, business acquaintances, even your friends need to feel comfortable about how you manage your life and your stewardship over your assets because these things reflect your values.

Think for a moment about your money management personality. If you are an extravagant spender and must always have the latest and best of everything, material things can eventually cloud your spiritual judgment. Your values can be moved from God to acquiring more things of the world.

What are the strengths of the extravagant spender that help as you seek your financial freedom? Once extravagant spenders know what they want and get focused, there is no stopping them. That same tenacity can be used to move toward financial freedom.

Your spending profile may not be extravagant, but there are still things you can improve on. What aspects of your personality affect how you perceive material things and the value of money? Are there strengths you can focus on to help get your financial life in better shape so you can pay more attention to your life's bigger purpose? What aspects of your personality tend to lead you into financial distress? Acknowledge them, give them to God and move forward with God's help. It is worth the investment because others may be watching. The way we manage money is a reflection of the things we value most in life, and the people around us observe our behavior.

Your financial decisions can have the ripple effect of a pebble thrown into a pond. Whether you are responsible or irresponsible will influence your spouse, your children, your family, your friends and coworkers. There is no question that your financial values affect your relationships. The question you must ask yourself is: Are my values having a positive or negative effect?

The next questions are, "Where do I go from here?" and "How do I create a foundation to move to a better place?" Remember God has not changed; He is waiting for us to seek out His direction to capture our vision and pursue our purpose. God wants us to be all we can be as His children.

If we eliminate some of the negative habits in our lives, we can progress to financial freedom for the long term, not just the short term.

If you're not satisfied with where your life is going, through faith, you can always find a new vision and new direction. It is never too late to change. And remember, the greatest form of worship is becoming all we can be and fulfilling God's purpose for our lives. God can use a changed heart. He can renew your spirit.

NOTES

A Faith Foundation to Financial Freedom

CHANGE YOUR BEHAVIOR.

Create in me a clean heart, O God;

and renew a right spirit within me.

Cast me not away from thy presence;

and take not thy Holy Spirit from me.

Restore unto me the joy

of Thy salvation

and uphold me with thy free spirit.

— Psalm 51:10-12

NOTES

CHANGE YOUR BEHAVIOR.

---------------- ✂️ ----------------

Each day we must get up with a renewed vitality to change our behavior as we seek financial freedom. What behaviors that hamper your success can you eliminate? If your spending style is overly emotional and you want to pay everyone else's bills, but you haven't paid your own, that's a behavior you can change.

A woman recently shared that she was desperately trying to change her behavior. Each month she loaned money to her coworkers even though she did not have it to loan. Her bills were growing farther behind. She couldn't take hearing a sad story and would always cover someone else if they asked her. Her prayer was for God to help her change, to remove the dependency that others had on her financially. She began offering strategic financial planning advice to her coworkers. This change in her behavior helped both her and her friends.

If your money management personality is extravagant, you, too, can change your behavior. Grounded in faith, you can learn to control your wants and expectations. Extravagant spenders get stuck in the "now" dilemma. They think, "I want what I want and I want it now!" They are so inclined to immediate gratification that they can't put off buying things. Whether it's pride, selfishness or just "keeping up with the Joneses," they get caught in the trap of satisfying all their wants, even if they are having difficulty handling their needs, and they wind up deep in debt.

Grounded in faith,
you can learn to control
your wants and expectations.

Our celebrity-focused society and the media have bombarded us with often unreasonable lifestyle expectations. Music, television and movie stars have expensive homes, jewelry, clothes and cars. Videos and reality shows promote the idea that a man needs lots of money to attract women and that women won't be bothered with men unless they have money.

Everyone wants the latest styles. As a young man, I wanted the latest car. Now it's a plasma screen television. But that doesn't mean I could—or should—satisfy those wants immediately. Not long ago, my son was with me at a shopping mall and he began asking me to buy him a Burberry shirt that cost more than $200. I knew it would just land on the floor like his $5 T-shirts! What kind of values would I teach him if I gave in and bought it for him and he didn't have to save or make a sacrifice for what he wants? We do our kids a disservice if we give in to their immediate gratification urges, whether we can afford to or not.

You may remember an episode of Bill Cosby's show when one of his daughters came home whining that other girls teased her about being rich because she had a nice house. Cosby told her not to worry about it, saying something to the effect of, "This is *my* house! *You* have no money!"

ANALYZE YOUR REAL VALUES.

I have traveled to South America, Europe and Africa. In these places, people think the citizens of the United States are wasteful. Small wonder they see our values as shallow and materialistic. Our conspicuous consumption of luxury goods reflects little spiritual depth.

If you are ignoring basic values, living for now and overlooking the need to save and plan for the future, I encourage you to see "now" in a different light, as "Need-or-Want," and examine spending, saving and debt accumulation in that light.

Your "wants" expenses may include money you spend on hobbies, travel, clothes, household items, gifts, eating out and entertainment, such as tickets to movies, concerts or sporting events. But as the old saying goes, not everything that looks good *to* you is good *for* you.

If you'll look closely at your discretionary spending, you'll find many places where you can distinguish between a need and a want.

- You need a new pair of shoes, but you only want them to be name brand.

- You need to get to work, but do you want to drive by yourself or could you carpool or use public transportation to save money?

- Do you really need a new DVD player, gold jewelry or designer clothes or do you just want them because someone else has them?

- Do you need to impress friends with a lavish night out or could you invest just as much in the relationships by taking them on a picnic or to a free concert?

- Do you make peer-pressured spending decisions or rational, well thought-out spending choices?

- Are you making what I call "value-added decisions" for your family and for your future? Why are you so focused on the now and not on the future? This says something about our society and not wanting to wait for anything.

Think about more economical ways of doing things. Determining what drives your short-term wants can help you get a handle on them and allow you to save money you can invest.

The choices we make as we work to build our lives are very important. Will I seek God in prayer and supplication? Will I educate myself on sound financial principles? Many of us did not learn these principles while growing up. Therefore, it is our responsibility to seek good financial guidance as adults. Saying we didn't know is clearly not the answer. We can't blame others for our adult choices.

DEAL WITH CREDIT CARD ADDICTION.

For some people spending or shopping becomes like an addiction similar to alcohol abuse, overeating or compulsive gambling. Resisting a purchase is difficult when a wallet full of credit cards makes buying something easy. For such people, the kind of "high" they get from spending is like drinking. But remember, there's always the headache the next morning!

If credit card spending to satisfy your wants has become an addiction for you, let me offer these six simple steps to help you overcome your habit:

1. Admit you have become powerless over your spending and have let your life become unmanageable.

2. Make the decision to turn your life over to the Creator as you understand Him, and draw the line in the sand to start now—not tomorrow or later this year—to make a change in your habits.

3. Be brutally honest with the person in the mirror. Make a list of why you have let your wants control your life.

4. Don't look for a short-term answer. You didn't get into the situation overnight and you may not be able to get out of it quickly either.

5. Take a daily personal inventory to examine how you can improve upon things you do.

6. Make a spiritual commitment to yourself to monitor your attitudes and perceptions about what you value and what you really want from life.

There is always time to change and there is always room for change. Ask God to create a clean heart in you and help you to change the things in your life that stand between you and financial fitness.

OVERCOME IMMEDIATE GRATIFICATION

I.   List three things you have purchased on impulse in the past year.

    1. _____

    2. _____

    3. _____

II. What is something you want that you are willing to wait for?

    _____

III. When you are tempted to give in to your wants, ask yourself:

    1. Why should I not make this purchase now?

       _____

       _____

       _____

    2. When can I reasonably afford this thing that I want rather than need?

       _____

       _____

    3. How can I plan to purchase this without credit?

       _____

       _____

       _____

    4. Does having this item help me in my life plan?

       _____

IV. Name at least two reasons you think you sometimes put wants before needs.

    1. _____

    2. _____

NOTES

A Faith Foundation to Financial Freedom

Hone your skills.

Study to shew thyself approved unto God,

a workman that needeth not to be ashamed,

rightly dividing the Word of truth.

— II Timothy 2:15

NOTES

A Faith Foundation to Financial Freedom

Hone your skills.

───────────── ⚜ ─────────────

Developing money management skills is an art, like anything else. Do not be embarrassed if you are still developing these skills.

Have you ever heard someone say, "I just don't know where the money goes"? Maybe you've said that yourself. A good first step before approaching financial goals is an in-depth assessment of where your income is going.

Be careful how you handle cash. One morning I left the house with $50 in my wallet. At the end of the day, it was gone! I started to think back to see what happened to it. I'd bought $10 of gasoline in the morning and spent about $3.50 on a fast breakfast, $30 on a business lunch and about $5.50 when I stopped by the drug store on the way home. Whoosh! Practically $50 just disappeared.

Keep a spending diary.

The best way to see where you're spending your money is to keep a spending diary. Do it for 30 days, religiously. Care enough about your plan to document everything. Write down exactly what you've spent either as you spend it or each night before going to bed. Include everything from coffee at the office to groceries, gasoline or any other shopping you do. Add your utility bills and credit card purchases. Account for every way you spend your money, from rent to chewing gum.

Until you know where your money is going, it will be difficult to set realistic goals.

After a month, you'll really know where your money has been going, down to the smallest thing, and you can begin to focus on areas where you can make some changes that will improve your spending and savings plans. You might discover, for example, that you're spending about $40 a week for lunches out of the office. Making your own lunches might save you half that. Over a year's time, that change alone could add up to $1,000 you could put away in savings or use to pay off a credit card.

Until you know where your money is going, it will be difficult to set realistic goals. But once you have an understanding of your spending habits, you will be prepared to make adjustments that will make a difference in both the short term and the long run.

Save it and bank it.

You can save without even having a bank account. That piggy bank at home is one way to start. The first accounts most people open at a bank or credit union are passbook savings accounts and checking accounts. These are easy to set up. Minors can have these accounts if adults cosign. We should teach our children early in life about managing money matters.

Thanks to the Federal Deposit Insurance Corporation (FDIC), deposits are insured for up to $100,000 at a single institution, so there's no need to fear trusting your funds to a bank. Although minimum balances may be required on checking accounts to avoid monthly fees, there is no risk involved in checking accounts or passbook savings. Some checking accounts even pay a small interest. Ask your banker about these first and take advantage of them if they are available.

You can use your checking account as your cash flow management system. It's simply a written record of what comes in and what goes out—your income and expenses. You may want to keep closer tabs on your bank accounts by using online banking services or by learning to use a personal accounting program you can run on your computer. Online banking and electronic funds transfers can make it easy to track your current balances and make transactions, but they don't substitute for having a face-to-face relationship with a banker with whom you can discuss your financial goals and from whom you can get advice when you want to move beyond checking and saving accounts.

Here are some tips about checking:

- Write down every check and ATM withdrawal.

- Avoid ATM withdrawals as much as possible, especially if they incur fees.

- Keep a running balance if not with each check, at least weekly. (Or check your balance online weekly.)

- Reconcile your statement every month without fail.

- Closely guard your checking account number codes, your ATM pin and your savings passbook.

- Learn what benefits and extras your bank offers with checking and savings accounts.

Whether you track your expenses on paper or by using a computer, tracking is the first skill you can master on the road to financial fitness.

KNOW WHERE YOUR MONEY GOES

I.   Begin your 30-day spending diary tomorrow. Use the sample below to get started.

II. Check with your bank to see whether an interest-bearing checking account is available.

III. Determine how often you used your ATM card in the past six months. Resolve to use it only half as much for the next six months.

IV. If you do not have savings other than a 401K, find out the minimum balance you need to open a passbook account at your bank or purchase a certificate of deposit. Compare the interest rates available.

Sample Spending Diary

Day	Expense	Cash	Check	Charge
Monday	Breakfast	$ 3.50		
	Soda at breakfast	$ .75		
	Lunch	$ 6.23		
	Blouse on sale at mall		$ 28.13	
	Drinks/friends after work	$ 9.50		
Tuesday	Gasoline			$16.00
	Roll and coffee at break	$ 3.75		
	Lunch	$10.00		
	Magazines at bookstore	$10.72		
	Shower gift for friend			$24.00
	Dinner out			$18.12
Wednesday	Coffee at work	$ 1.00		
	Newspaper	$ .50		
	Video rental	$ 4.00		
	Pizza			$20.00
	Sodas for pizza night	$ 3.95		
Thursday	Breakfast	$ 3.50		
	Lunch	$ 7.50		
	Paid Rent		$550.00	
	Check for book club dues		$ 35.00	
	Groceries		$ 58.28	
Friday	Breakfast with book club	$ 8.00		
	Concert ticket	$43.00		
	Dinner with friends	$24.00		

NOTES

A Faith Foundation to Financial Freedom

OPERATE FROM INTEGRITY.

And this I pray, that your love may abound
yet more and more in knowledge
and in all judgment;
That ye may approve things
that are excellent;
that ye may be sincere and without offense
until the day of Christ;
Being filled with the fruits of righteousness,
which are by Jesus Christ,
unto the glory and praise of God.
— Philippians 1: 9-11

NOTES

OPERATE FROM INTEGRITY.

Integrity for believers of God is an awesome responsibility. Our financial integrity carries a heavier weight because it can also be a public testimony. Do you deliver what you promised when you promised it? Your integrity lives in what I call your financial DNA. When a report is given about how you operate financially, will it be a straight line to results or a loop of overcommitment and limited delivery? Personal integrity is at the core of financial fitness.

Liz, one of the nicest people I know, has worked with me on numerous projects in faith-based financing. Although she is honest, she always misses her deadlines, causing others around her to hustle to make up for her missteps. A banker recently questioned me about her integrity as a business partner. When Liz and I discussed her perpetual tardiness, she explained that she was very committed; she had just gotten busy and was over extended. When she realized this was affecting her integrity and the way she was being viewed, she immediately changed. Your reputation is all you have. *People judge your integrity by what they see, not what you say.*

Another way to operate in integrity is through your credit rating. It is amazing in today's marketplace how often a credit rating is being used to approve people or weed them out. Each of the money management personalities approaches credit differently. Calculated spenders may check their credit rating monthly. An extravagant spender may never think about it. The realistic spender understands the value of credit. The emotional spender may worry about it and may be afraid to deal with it.

Your credit rating is your credibility when you are applying for loans or credit. When I got into financial trouble, I learned the hard way that a problem with your credit rating causes you to pay higher interest and takes a long time to overcome. It's an exceptional saver—or a person with a very high income—who has enough money to buy cars or homes outright. Although we might save enough for the down payments, most of us depend on credit to make those major purchases. When you apply for a home mortgage or a loan to buy a car, one of the first things the lender does is pull your credit report. The lenders may tell you that you don't qualify but they usually won't divulge what they found in your report. So it's important to do what you can to maintain or clean up your credit rating.

CONFRONT YOUR CREDIT RATING.

People are often afraid to confront their fears about their credit ratings. As I speak around the country, I find people who don't want to look at their credit reports. I asked a person I was helping with financing a home, "Why were you so afraid to have me look at your credit?"

She replied, "I have had some things happen in my past with respect to my credit that I am not proud of and I didn't want you to think negatively of me." She felt her integrity would be questioned. I explained that if she did not face it and put together a plan to address her credit, she could not move forward.

When I saw her credit report, it wasn't as bruised as she thought. We put together a step-by-step plan to get her back on track:

- We closed all the open accounts she had not used and that held high lines of credit.

- We wrote letters to companies that had reported incorrect information about her accounts, making them aware of the Fair Credit Act and obligating them to report her account information to the credit bureaus properly.

- She wrote to all the credit agencies to notify them of her process of getting those things cleared up on her credit standing.

- She put dates on her calendar to check her own credit report to ensure changes had been made and new information was correct.

In the United States, the credit tracking process is dominated by three big companies:

- Equifax, 800-437-4951, www.equifax.com,
  PO Box 105139, Atlanta GA 30348

- Experian, 888-397-3742, www.experian.com,
  955 American Lane, Schaumburg IL 60173

- TransUnion, 800-916-8800, www.transunion.com,
  PO Box 2000, Chester PA 19022

Different lenders, such as department stores, bank credit cards and mortgage and car companies, report to these bureaus. You can purchase a report of your own credit from one bureau or get a combined report from all three if you want to see how your credit rating is being reported. Simply call or log onto one of the Web sites to order a review of your own credit.

A new federal law allows consumers to access their own credit reports annually for no charge.

If you are turned down for credit, you are entitled to a free copy of your credit report. Occasionally errors are made— when your name is the same as someone else's, for instance, or for other reasons, including identity theft. If you find errors on your report, you can submit challenges or explanations to facilitate corrections and clear inaccuracies from your credit statement. You should review your own credit report from time to time to ensure that everything is correct.

A new federal law, the Fair and Accurate Credit Transactions Act, allows consumers to access their own credit reports annually for no charge. To get a free report, you can call the Central Source at 1-877-322-8228 or you can go to www.annualcreditreport.com.

Looking at your own report from time to time is advice I've been giving for years. Even when you have to pay a fee, it is worth it to pull your own credit report.

The big three credit bureaus have Web sites that give you information about how to read your reports. Be aware that reporting may be entered on 30, 60, 90 or 120-day cycles. If you make late payments two times 30 days late or three times 60 days late, that will drive your credit score down. Generally, the fewer times you make late payments, the better your score.

Be aware that there are other Internet sites that offer you credit reports for fees. Some charge more than you need to pay, so start with the three reporting bureaus and remember you can now get at least one report a year for no charge.

UNDERSTAND YOUR CREDIT SCORE.

The Fair Isaac Corporation (FICO) uses credit bureau reports to tabulate FICO scores ranging from 300 to 850 that gauge your credit-worthiness. The higher the FICO score, the better credit risk you are and the greater likelihood of receiving a loan. Mortgage companies may offer more favorable interest rates to those who have higher FICO scores. If you have a low credit rating, you may have to pay a higher interest rate than someone who has a better credit score, so it is worth it to establish a good credit rating through your bank loan or credit card payments. Lenders take risks when they loan money, so they charge higher interest rates if the credit history indicates there may be problems with repayment.

The bureaus have different names for FICO scores. At Equifax, it's Beacon; at Experian, it's Isaac Risk Score; at TransUnion, it's Empirica.

Here are the elements of your credit that are analyzed in compiling your credit score:

- The number of credit obligations you have. These may include bank, department store and gasoline credit cards as well as home, car and student loans.

- Your payment performance. According to FICO, only 10 percent of the population has ever defaulted on a loan or credit account, and only 15 percent have ever had an account more than 90 days overdue. But if you are in those groups, your payment record can negatively affect your report.

- Credit utilization. Although about half of credit card holders carry less than $1,000 balance, almost 30 percent have more than $10,000 of debt, not including a mortgage, say FICO's statistics.

- Total available credit can impact your credit score. You may not realize that the combined limits of all your credit cards can be a negative. Even if you're using only $1,000 on a credit card, if your credit limit is $10,000, that's the amount credit scorers may consider to be your risk level. And you'll be judged on the high limit rather than what you're actually using. Make sure your card's credit limit is no more than double the amount you'll normally charge each month. This decreases your risk both personally in how you manage your credit and in the eyes of the creditors.

- Length of credit history. Having well-established credit over a period of time means you have been managing well and can be trusted to manage well in the future.

- Inquiries. When you apply for credit or when an authorized entity checks your credit, it is posted as a query to your file. Too many queries may mean you are seeking a lot of credit, and that can be a red flag to lenders.

Although credit histories look at the types of financial obligations you have and how you have handled them over time, they do not address other factors such as age, gender, race, religion or marital status. Nor do they consider your checking and savings accounts or interest rates on your debts. Although your address and current employment are included on your credit report for identification, your occupation, your salary and where you live are not relevant to your calculated FICO score.

ESTABLISH AND GUARD YOUR CREDIT.

Maybe you have never had credit but want to get a loan. How can you prove to a lender that you are a good steward and deserve the loan? If you don't have a bank account, you can give references from a landlord, who will vouch you have always paid your rent on time. Or you can show a year's worth of utility bills, phone payments or similar receipts to help establish your credibility. Some lenders will take your pay stubs as verification of a level of income. But be careful. Some lenders who talk about taking almost anything to help finance a new car, for example, may be charging very high interest rates.

If you do have a bank account, talk with your banker about extending you a line of credit or using your CD as collateral for a small personal loan. A small business loan or home improvement loan that you can pay off quickly also can help establish your credit. If you make regular, on-time payments on the loan at your bank, you will start establishing good credit. Your banker can also issue a credit card that will help establish your credit.

For good or bad, your credit rating is not permanent. It can fluctuate. If you fall behind on payments, it will be reflected in a lower FICO score. But if you get your credit debt in line—cancel some cards, pay off some debts, charge well below your limits and pay on time each month—you can improve your credit rating. Here are some things to remember about your credit rating:

- Don't build up your credit too quickly. It can send a negative message to lenders or scoring agencies.

- Do everything you can to avoid identity theft. Watch your mail. Shred financial information when it's not needed for your files. Don't give out your Social Security number unless you're sure it's necessary.

- Ask for special access codes or questions only you can provide the answers to.

- If your wallet or pocketbook is lost or stolen, notify all your credit card companies and your bank to be aware of possible identity theft. (Be sure to cancel all current credit cards and have new numbers issued.)

- Monitor your credit standing once or twice a year. This may enable you to catch errors or identity theft, a crime that is becoming more common. If you are denied credit, get a free copy of your credit report and check for errors.

- Eliminate outstanding debt through negotiating with lenders.

Just remember that your integrity may be judged by your practice of good or bad credit and spending habits. Don't charge more than you can handle and easily pay off in full each month. That way you can establish a good rating and gain a reputation for integrity.

Protect Your Credit Rating

I. List your credit cards and your current monthly balance on each card.

	Credit Cards	**Balance**
1.	_____	_____
2.	_____	_____
3.	_____	_____
4.	_____	_____
5.	_____	_____
6.	_____	_____
7.	_____	_____
8.	_____	_____
	TOTAL	_____

II. Get a current credit report on yourself by calling or contacting one of the three credit bureaus online. What is your current FICO score?

_____

III. Besides credit cards, list other debt obligations that are being tracked on your report. (cars, home, student loans, etc.)

1. _____

2. _____

3. _____

PROTECT YOUR CREDIT RATING (CONTINUED)

IV. List three things you can do in the next year to improve your score. (Pay off which card? Cancel which card?)

1. _____

2. _____

3. _____

V. Make sure that everything is correct on your report. List any discrepancies. Contact the bureau with your corrections.

1. _____

2. _____

3. _____

VI. Within the next week, collect all the contact information (like toll-free numbers or Web sites) for your credit cards and store it in a safe place so you can quickly cancel cards in case of loss, theft or identity theft issues.

VII. Resolve to make all payments on time and keep balances low over the next two years to improve your credit rating. What is your goal for your FICO score?

_____

NOTES

A Faith Foundation to Financial Freedom

OWN YOUR DECISIONS.

If we say that we have not sin,

we deceive ourselves,

and the truth is not in us.

If we confess our sins,

he is faithful and just to forgive us our sins,

and to cleanse us

from all unrighteousness.

— I John 1:8-9

NOTES

A Faith Foundation to Financial Freedom

Own your decisions.

cx80

Remember being at the movies as a kid and covering your eyes when you didn't want to watch something bad happen? I've known people who let their bills pile up but refuse to call creditors to work out a payment plan or to see a financial consultant to get help. But we can't be like ostriches with our heads in the sand. Things are happening around us even when we refuse to look at them.

Open your eyes.

Have you really taken a good look at what poor financial decisions are costing you? Here are just a few things that might be costing you more than you realize:

- High interest rates on your credit cards (often 18 percent to 22 percent or more)

- Late fees when payments aren't made on time (5 percent of total bill or more)

- Bounced check fees ($25 to $35 is not unusual.)

- Fees for not maintaining minimum balances ($4 to

$10 if less than $500 balance)

- Restart fees when services are cut and then reconnected (Reconnecting a cell phone because of canceled service for nonpayment)

- Advance check-cashing services (up to 10 percent of your check)

- Consolidation loans (Fees for services vary but can be costly.)

A woman in one of my focus groups summed up the issue of managing and saving money. "It's like trying to lose weight. Everyone knows what they should do—work at it and track their progress. It's really doing it and sticking with it that's the problem."

Have you really taken a good look at what poor financial decisions are costing you?

Knowledge is one thing. Application is another. Pulling your head out of the sand requires long-term, consistent application and is challenging. Lee Colan, a friend of mine, wrote a book called *Sticking to It: The Art of Adherence.* Lee says adherence to a plan is a product of focus, competence and passion. The great news is that if you have something going in each of those areas, the end result is exponential!

Do a reality check.

My first reality check came in a disastrous fashion 15 years ago. My business partner took advantage of my being too trusting. The reality check for me after that was to confront the brutal facts about doing business. I may not like the behind-the-scenes details of business, but my credit rating and my integrity were tarnished by one bad situation. My painful reality check left me feeling crushed, humiliated and discouraged. Yet, it also set me on the path to pursue the purpose I now enjoy. That is why I know God is still the author and finisher of our lives. He took my distraught reality and turned it into his platform for a purpose. Our God is an awesome God!

Perhaps your reality check will not be as painful as mine was, but you still need to walk through the process. Do you tend to be the one who always picks up the tab? Are you trying to use money to buy friendships or exert control? Do you lend money to friends, not knowing whether you'll ever see it again? Are you trying to compensate for some insecurity by purchasing things you could do without? Get real with yourself about your spending habits and how you use money in your relationships.

Eliminate the "poor me" mindset.

Getting in the right mindset is critical to managing your finances. First of all, you have to accept that spending and saving are conscious, voluntary choices you make, not things you are forced to do and have no control over.

When you are tempted to buy those expensive tennis shoes or that designer handbag, don't respond to yourself by saying, "I can't afford that." Instead of making it seem like you're being deprived, take a positive perspective and tell yourself, "I choose not to buy that because I'd rather have the money for my new car down payment" (or whatever else you're saving for). Do you see the difference? Your money is not controlling your choices.

You can choose to change your perception and control your financial fitness. And you can truly own your decisions because you want to grow in purpose with God.

Take Your Head Out of the Sand

I. How many times in the past three months have you paid a late fee, restart fee or bounced check fee? Total these and divide by three to get an average.

Late fees total   _____

Restart fees   _____

Check fees   _____

Total   _____ ÷ 3 = _____ (average per month)

II. Total the interest charges you were charged on all your credit cards for the past three months. Then average them.

Month 1   _____

Month 2   _____

Month 3   _____

Total   _____ ÷ 3 = _____ (average per month)

III. Add together the average per month charges in sections I. and II. above. Then multiply by 12 to see how much you could be losing over a year. (If you average $100 in fees or credit card interest per month, you could be losing $1,200 per year. That's $6,000 in five years!)

Question 1 Average   _____

Question 2 Average   _____

Total   _____ ÷ 2 = _____ x 12 = _____

IV. List every occasion when such charges occurred. Determine what you spent your money on that caused you to miss payments, make late payments or incur interest.

_____

_____

_____

NOTES

SELECT YOUR SUPPORT SYSTEM.

Finally, my brethren, be strong in the Lord,
and in the power of His might.
Put on the whole armour of God,
that ye may be able to stand
against the wiles of the devil.
For we wrestle not against flesh and blood,
but against principalities, against powers,
against the rulers of the darkness of this world,
against spiritual wickedness in high places.
Wherefore take unto you the whole armor
of God that ye may be able to withstand
in the evil day, and having done all to stand.
— Ephesians 6:10-13

NOTES

A Faith Foundation to Financial Freedom

SELECT YOUR SUPPORT SYSTEM.

—————— ◌ॐ◌ ——————

Who are the people in your life who help you to stand? When the Apostle Paul encourages us to put on the whole armor, it means you utilize every spiritual resource available to you. When you set out on your financial journey, there are key players who must be a part of your armor.

> **Your support system always starts with the people closest to you.**

First is your family. If you have a spouse, will he or she support your new journey to get the family financially fit? I often hear from couples that one person is working to get them out of debt while the other person is working just as hard to keep them in it. That will definitely hamper your progress. However, you may have the opportunity to become a financially fit role model for your spouse. Your support system always starts with the people closest to you.

Next, evaluate your relationship with your banker. Does your banker know you, or are you allowing total strangers to control your money? Build a relationship and watch the options grow.

FIND EXPERT GUIDANCE.

Do you have a person on your team to help with taxes? So many people become financially destitute because they do not get solid tax advice from a qualified tax specialist or CPA. As you improve your financial foundation and move from one tax bracket to another, this team support becomes increasingly important.

Depending on where you are in your financial journey, you may need people who can advise you about investing, such as a financial planner or a real estate advisor. Real estate continues to be one of the soundest investments we can make. Attorneys and insurance specialists may also be important team members to ensure your protection.

Evaluate where you are, where you want to begin making changes and step out on faith. It's amazing how often God will send the right support at just the right time.

RELY ON YOUR BANKER.

Your banker can be a valuable partner over the years. Having several types of accounts in your bank increases your ability to leverage your presence with the banker and help you get the most from your relationship, from eliminating fees to securing personalized attention for your concerns. You may start with your own checking or passbook savings account. As your needs change, you may turn to your banker for help with a variety of things:

- A savings account for your child
- Loans for college or special training
- Credit cards or lines of credit
- Loans for a growing business
- Advice for finding venture capital
- Certificates of deposit
- Savings bonds
- Car loans
- Home loans or home improvement loans
- Loans for luxury items such as a boat or a second home
- A safety deposit box to secure important papers or heirlooms
- A trust fund for the next generation

Your banker can be a great resource. If you meet your banker and grow to trust his judgment, you can talk to him or her about your dreams and plans. You can learn about the banker's experience with other clients, find out how things have been done by others and learn from their mistakes. The banker has the wisdom of the experiences of all the clients to draw from when advising you. You can learn from that stockpile of information before you take any risks yourself. It gives you the freedom to make well-informed decisions.

Most bankers also know about other investments and can advise you about them. They may know CPAs, tax attorneys or other professionals to refer you to and can steer you away from ones they know have lower reputations. Your banker is likely to be involved in community organizations that can benefit you and can make introductions to people you may need to know because of your business or personal objectives. In short, your banker can be a hub of a support team to help you build relationships to succeed and meet your goals.

BUILD A RELATIONSHIP WITH A BANKING PARTNER

I. What banking services do you currently use?

   1. _____

   2. _____

   3. _____

II. What banking services do you think you may need in the future that you are not using now?

   1. _____

   2. _____

   3. _____

   4. _____

III. If you currently have a banking account of some kind but do not know a loan officer or other bank advisor, find out the name of someone at your bank who can assist you. Write that individual's name and phone number here.

   Name _____

   Phone _____

IV. List two ways you think knowing a banker could be useful to helping you achieve your personal or business financial goals.

   1. _____

   2. _____

NOTES

A Faith Foundation to Financial Freedom

ELEVATE YOUR CONSCIOUSNESS.

Finally, Brethren,
whatsoever things are true,
whatsoever things are honest,
whatsoever things are just,
whatsoever things are pure,
whatsoever things are lovely,
whatsoever things are of good report;
if there be any virtue,
and if there be any praise,
think on these things.
— Philippians 4:4-8

NOTES

ELEVATE YOUR CONSCIOUSNESS.

Credit cards are a great convenience. The inventor of credit cards said he started them in the United States to enable ordinary people to take advantage of sales so they could save money. But, unfortunately, over time, credit card use often evolves into abuse. People may spend almost unconsciously and find themselves overextended in credit card debt that carries high interest. If you extend your credit card spending to achieve your chosen lifestyle, rather than doing reasonable financial management and planning, you will find the side effects can be devastating.

You may not be aware of the many ways your money management can affect your life. Some employers are now checking credit reports of job applicants. They assume that people in debt not only experience stress but also may succumb to the temptation to embezzle. Some insurance companies are charging more to insure people with debt problems, citing more frequent claims by those who have credit issues to deal with. Even if you consider yourself the most honest person in the world, people who make decisions involving your life use your credit worthiness as a gauge of your character and responsibility.

Avoid the stress of debt.

Debt is like a shackle that binds our society. It is an enemy of a comfortable lifestyle. Being in debt is not comfortable. "Debt causes stress," say the folks we've spoken to in focus groups. And the stress can be physical as well as emotional. Fear of bill collectors puts people on edge. Debt may make it difficult to concentrate at work. The stress can cause higher blood pressure.

The danger of being in debt is that it's hard to get out. You find yourself creating another debt to pay off the first one; you rob Peter to pay Paul, but something is always left hanging.

It's easy to see that credit card debt creates a problem that is difficult to overcome. One woman I spoke with had bottomed out in credit card debt. She had gone too far and finally sought help. She is not using credit cards for anything these days. And she expects it will take her two more years, living very conservatively, to pay off all her old credit card debt.

If you can't pay your credit card balance off in full each month, you can't afford to say, "Charge it!"

Unfortunately, some people in her situation repeat the cycle. They pay all their credit cards down and then start filling them up again. The best advice is that if you can't pay your credit card balance off in full each month, you can't afford to say, "Charge it!"

Just as the beneficial power of compounded interest is evident in savings accounts, it becomes a powerful and dangerous force when it is charged against your credit card debt. Suppose you made monthly payments against a $5,000 credit card balance without ever charging another thing to the account. Here's how it would work out:

Balance	Interest Rate	Monthly Payment	Paid Off In	Total $ Paid
$5,000	18%	$100	93 months (7 years, 9 months)	$9,300
$5,000	18%	$200	32 months (2 years, 8 months)	$6,400

Remember, this chart shows what happens if you never add a single charge to the $5,000! Credit card spending can be a big temptation or a great convenience. How you handle it is up to you. It can add value to your life or it can add stress and panic.

There is so much more to credit card debt than money and stress. It is not uncommon for uncontrolled credit card spending to break up a marriage. Here are some things people we surveyed say about how debt affects their lifestyle:

- I have no free-spending funds. All my paycheck goes to bills.

- I'm always down and out trying to figure out my next move toward paying bills.

- All of the money I make goes to paying off my debt. I have absolutely no disposable income.

- I can't go shopping, can't take trips. There are arguments with my spouse.

- Shopping at Wal-Mart instead of Macy's. I have to find inexpensive ways to do things.

- Creates stress. Affects relationships with family.

If you value your relationships and your own well-being, you'll work to ensure that debt is minimized and solid financial thinking replaces it.

CONQUER CREDIT CARD SPENDING.

Considering the costs of carrying credit card debt with high interest rates and the emotional stress of such debt—not to mention how that stress may overflow into all the areas of your life—it seems logical not to fall victim to credit card spending. Some people have to learn the hard way that, rather than enhancing the quality of your life, credit card misuse saps the value from your life.

Many credit card companies start marketing to young people when they reach 18 or enter college, when self-discipline is not well established. It's a time when that urge for instant gratification is hard to resist. Of course, just because credit is offered, does not mean you have to accept it. Being young doesn't mean you can't make smart choices. Age is not always the gauge of maturity. You can learn early or late what may affect you for a lifetime.

On a recent visit to a university campus, I asked a group of students about credit cards. Almost 95 percent of them had credit cards and half already had debt over $5,000. One person said she had over $10,000 in debt but she couldn't remember what she had spent all that money on. I thought, "That much money could have bought a car!" I believe young adults of college age should never have more than one or two credit cards and should have limits not exceeding $500.

Regardless of your age, it helps if you understand the motivation behind your being offered credit. Rather than thinking of your convenience, credit card companies:

- See an opportunity to make money off your spending by charging you interest

- Want to make a profit on other products or services they offer

- Take advantage of the Need-Or-Want mentality

Some older adults have never explored the roots of their excessive spending. They, too, need to approach credit cards with discipline. Here are a few pointers to help conquer credit card problems:

- Read every contract carefully before signing. Take time to understand what you're getting into.

- Keep all documentation so you can go back and

read what you have signed in reference to your credit cards.

- Charge only what you can pay for at the end of the month. Paying your balance every month allows you to avoid finance charges.

- Analyze your bills for mistakes and overcharges.

- Pay your bills on time. Late payments incur penalties as well as interest charges. Watch for your statement each month and be sure one is not missing or skipped.

- Think carefully before accepting an offer to increase your credit line. Never carry a total line of credit on all your credit cards that is higher than your annual salary. (Although you may think having a high line of credit would be handy if you were to lose your job, lenders see it as a liability, a potential for you to "max out" your cards and be unable to pay.)

- Consider using only one credit card. Out of all your cards, is there a low-interest one you could consolidate all the others to? Or can you pay off a smaller credit card debt so you could add the dollars onto the payment of another card?

- If you choose to roll over credit card balances to a less expensive card, be sure to pay off the balance quickly before a higher rate kicks in.

- If you roll over a card to another or decide to stop using a card, contact the company to officially cancel the card you won't be using. Otherwise, the credit line may still work against your rating.

- Use no more than 50 percent of your credit limit. Do not raise your limit if your income is reduced.

- Monitor your credit availability and balances at least once a quarter.

- Cancel any credit cards you are not using. (Don't just cut them up!)

- Shred any new credit card offers that come in the mail.

Increasing your knowledge of how credit spending can work against your long-term financial goals will help you make more conscious choices about money management.

Avoid the Dangers of Credit Card Debt

I. How credit cards affect my lifestyle.

Positive effects	Negative effects
1. _____	_____
2. _____	_____
3. _____	_____

II. List the credit cards you (and your significant other) currently hold, their annual or monthly fees and the interest rates.

Card	Fee	Interest rate
1. _____	_____	_____
2. _____	_____	_____
3. _____	_____	_____
4. _____	_____	_____
5. _____	_____	_____
6. _____	_____	_____
7. _____	_____	_____
8. _____	_____	_____

III. What is your current total credit card limit?

_____

IV. What is your current total credit card debt?

_____

A Faith Foundation to Financial Freedom

PART 4

YOUR FUTURE

...but this one thing I do,
forgetting those things
which are behind,
and reaching forth unto those things
which are before,
I press toward the mark for the prize
of the high calling of God in Christ Jesus.
— Philippians 3:13-14

NOTES

A Faith Foundation to Financial Freedom

Part 4

Your Future

For many years it was easy to look back and regret my big financial mistake. One day a pastor told me, "God has forgiven you. Forgive yourself and focus on your purpose." That was a real turning point for me. I realized I had to create a constant focus on my financial growth. I had to discipline myself and seek a new level of financial fitness. The first step for me was to consult a financial planner. Many people think they cannot afford one. I would say you can't afford not to have one. A financial planner can help evaluate the habits you have from your past, the goals you want for your future and your plans to get there.

Glenda, who attended our financial institute, used a planner to change her future when a divorce left her destitute and in debt. The planner advised her to develop the habit of saving. At the time she could save only $50 a month. The financial planner helped to evaluate the decisions she had made in the past and set her on a course for better decision making. She began to make better choices. She said her guide to change her future was set in Matthew 6:33, "But seek first the kingdom of God and His righteousness and all these things shall be added unto you." That was the scripture God gave her over and over again. She now pays her tithe and saves a tenth each month. She owns a home and has limited bills. The plan worked for her.

Wherever you are now, you have the opportunity to refocus and address your financial future. Trusting in God to help you, you can leave the past behind and build a firmer foundation based on faith.

Stay focused.

> *Teach me, O Lord, the way of thy statutes;*
> *and I shall keep it unto the end.*
> *Give me understanding,*
> *and I shall keep thy law;*
> *yea, I shall observe it with my whole heart.*
> *Make me go in the path*
> *of thy commandments;*
> *for therein do I delight.*
> *— Psalms 119:33-35*

NOTES

A Faith Foundation to Financial Freedom

Stay focused.

———— ✂ ————

We all know that the habits we start early in life tend to stay with us. So it's a good idea for parents who have good financial management skills to pass that wisdom on to their children. A fellow I know has a couple of children who earn money doing odd jobs around the neighborhood, mowing yards, raking leaves and that kind of thing. He requires them to practice a 30/70 plan. They set aside 10 percent of their earnings for the church, 10 percent for short-term savings (like when they want to buy something expensive or put away money for buying Christmas gifts) and 10 percent for long-term (their college funds). Then they are free to spend the other 70 percent of their money on everyday things.

Many of us did not grow up with the benefit of that kind of teaching from a parent who is disciplined about money matters. Some learn in high school or college. It's good for young adults to start learning financial management and developing plans of their own about what they want and how they will get there. Others have to learn over time and come to money wisdom a little later, but you can train yourself and start setting good financial management goals regardless of your age.

The old saying goes, "Failing to plan is planning to fail." Your plan must include spending and saving strategies.

> *You can train yourself*
> *and start setting good financial*
> *management goals*
> *regardless of your age.*

DEVELOP A SPENDING STRATEGY.

The basis of your spending strategy is your budget. You should be able to establish a budget that will help you accomplish your goals. Divide your budget into three categories:

1. Obligations that are always the same amount may include:

   - Mortgage
   - Car payment
   - Commuting fares or parking
   - Childcare
   - Child support payments
   - College loan payments
   - Insurance

- Regular prescriptions
- Your church pledge
- Cable TV

2. Recurring expenses that vary every month, such as:

- Utilities
- Food
- Gasoline
- Clothes
- Phone bill

If you are paying for insurance quarterly or once a year, be sure to divide the expense and count it monthly. Car maintenance and home upkeep should be estimated monthly, too.

3. Discretionary expenses. These are the things you don't have to have but are usually spending money on, such as:

- Movies
- Concerts
- Sporting events
- Travel
- Magazines
- Gifts
- Eating out
- Cigarettes
- Drinking
- Bingo
- Lottery tickets

With some discipline and an eye on the big picture, you can learn to control some of your discretionary expenses and put the money in savings to work for you and help you accomplish long-term goals. In fact, you may even find ways to save in the first two categories. You can cut down on the money you spend on clothes, for example, or discontinue your cable TV subscription.

Some people do not have a regular, reliable income. Seasonal workers, salespeople on commission and those who run their own businesses may experience highs and lows in their income. Someone who runs a landscaping service may have more income in the warmer months, for example, while a heating and air conditioning specialist may have more work in the winter. A retail salesperson may expect more income around the holidays, while a real estate agent might have better income in the spring and fall. These people must plan in the high times to compensate for the low times.

CREATE A SAVINGS STRATEGY.

Your savings strategy is an outgrowth of your budget. It's essential when you build your budget that you put savings in the first category—as a regular, set expense that is never omitted—and work to increase the amount you set as your savings obligation. Many people consider it "paying themselves first." People I surveyed saved an average of 8.5 percent of their income, including what they put in their 401Ks at their employment. But a large percentage of Americans have no savings at all! Here are some simple ways to get started:

- If you have never had a savings plan, you may need to begin with small increments. Perhaps you can decide to give up smoking and put all the money you spent on that habit into savings. Maybe you can forego the cost of eating out at least once a week or do without some magazine subscriptions to have money to set aside for the future. Some people even use ideas like saving all the quarters they get or all the $5 bills. Little things will add up, and once you get started, you will find additional ways to save instead of spend.

- For many people, automatic transfers and payroll deductions are great plans. If you never see the money, you don't miss it. The majority of people I've spoken to participate in 401K plans offered through their jobs, taking advantage of tax benefits and automatic deductions. If the company you work for offers matching contributions, even better. Of course, a 401K is for long-term investing, not short-term goals or emergencies. You can't withdraw from a 401K without risking penalties. That's the reason it should help you resist the temptation to use it before the proper time.

- Investigate tax-free municipal bonds or other investments in the bond market. Find out about programs where you can invest pre-tax dollars for your childrens' education. There may be ways you can contribute to a health care plan or other ways to invest in yourself while saving money you might otherwise pay out in taxes.

- Another interesting plan to increase your nest egg is to put into savings any money that you get from raises or bonuses. Since you've gotten used to living on what you were making, investing any increase or windfall can help you get on the road to a savings commitment, even if it's only two or three percent of your income.

- Your bank may offer automatic transfers from your checking account into your savings account. Establish a relationship with your banker and ask what types of programs are available to make it easier for you to accumulate savings and help manage your goals. A good advisor can help you plan where you want to be in a year, five years, and 20 years from now.

- Once you've established your savings accounts, work hard to make those funds—whether passbook savings, certificates of deposit, or individual retirement accounts—strictly off limits except for their intended purposes. Resist the temptation to take money out of your child's college fund for car repairs.

A good savings plan adds value to your work efforts and reaps rewards of security and peace because you know you have a cushion to fall back on in case of a true emergency. The earlier you start, the better, but it's never too late to get a better mindset about money management, set new budgets or practice better saving habits. Bring more value to your life by staying focused on your spending and saving goals.

DEVELOP A PLAN OF ACTION

I. Start your monthly budget. Transfer it to a notebook or spreadsheet.

Stable Obligations (Ex. Rent, Car, Child Care)	**Variable Expenses** (Ex. Electricity, Food, Gas)	**Discretionary** (Ex. Movies, Dining out, Gifts)	**Savings** (Ex. 401K, Bank, Other)
_____	_____	_____	_____
_____	_____	_____	_____
_____	_____	_____	_____
_____	_____	_____	_____
_____	_____	_____	_____
_____	_____	_____	_____

Totals   _____   _____   _____   _____

II. List three areas of discretionary spending where you can find money to save or invest. (For example, skip eating out two times at $15 each and put the $30 in savings.)

   1. _____
   2. _____
   3. _____

III. What percentage of your salary do you currently save?

IV. Ask your employer about participating (or increasing your participation) in a 401K.

V. Check with your banker or financial advisor about an IRA (individual retirement account).

VI. Ask your banker about moving your passbook savings to a CD or other account with higher interest rates.

VII. Consider a savings partner. Work together with someone you trust to help motivate you to save.

NOTES

A Faith Foundation to Financial Freedom

𝒰

UNDERSTAND RISKS AND REWARDS.

That the God of our Lord Jesus Christ,
the Father of glory,
may give unto you the spirit of wisdom
and revelation in the knowledge of Him;
The eyes of your understanding
being enlightened; that ye may know
what is the hope of His calling,
and what the riches of the glory
of His inheritance in the saints.
And what is the exceeding greatness
of His power to usward who believe,
according to the working of His might power.
— Ephesians 1:17-19

NOTES

Understand risks and rewards.

Financial advisors talk about "risk tolerance." That refers to how comfortable you are risking your money in attempting to get higher returns. Generally, the younger you are, the more you can afford to take a risk, but your financial portfolio should become more conservative as you get older. You want to protect what you have accumulated when you have less time left to earn it back.

Everyone discovered in the past few years just how risky stocks can be. Headlines shouted losses in the stock market and scandals in retirement accounts at companies such as Enron.

Take advantage of compounding interest.

Savings, CDs and many other bank savings products traditionally have been viewed as safe investments. Because they are not high-risk, they tend not to be high-yield. But don't overlook the power of saving, even if you have a low risk tolerance and want to avoid riskier investments such as stocks.

Suppose you start with $50 in an investment earning 6.5 percent interest, compounded monthly. Then you add $50 each month without fail. If you could manage to double those amounts at the same interest and compounding rates, the money would accumulate much faster.

Investing at a steady rate over time reaps rewards.

Either way, after 30 years, you'd still have more than three times your total investment, thanks to compounding interest. Here's how it works out:

Start With	Add per month	10 yrs. invested	10 yrs. return	20 yrs. invested	20 yrs. return	30 yrs. invested	30 yrs. return
$50	$50	$6,000	$8,516	$12,000	$24,704	$18,000	$55,658
$100	$100	$12,000	$17,032	$24,000	$49,408	$36,000	$111,317

It's easy to see how investing at a steady rate over time reaps rewards. Some investments may yield more than 6.5 percent compounded monthly; some will earn less.

THINK BEYOND A PASSBOOK SAVINGS ACCOUNT.

A passbook savings account is the most basic kind of savings instrument. Because your funds are accessible for withdrawal at any time, passbook accounts usually pay lower interest rates than other options that require you to deposit your money for a specified time. (In 2005, passbook savings accounts generally earn less than 2 percent.) Although you can withdraw funds from some of the more sophisticated investment products, a penalty is incurred. Think of it as the price you pay for not keeping your end of the commitment.

Other common savings/investment options include:

- Certificates of deposit (CDs)
- Money market accounts
- Savings bonds
- Treasury notes
- Municipal bonds
- Mutual funds
- Stocks
- Tax-deferred retirement accounts
- Individual retirement accounts

Of course, a banker or financial advisor can counsel you about the types of accounts that are best for you, whatever your situation or age. Understand the risks and rewards of various kinds of investments. It can help you choose the best ways to protect and grow your money to achieve your financial fitness goals.

ANALYZE RISK AND RETURNS

I.   Are you a natural risk-taker?

_____

II. What degree of risk can you reasonably afford?

_____

III. Write an example of when you have taken a risk or refused to take one. What were the results?

_____

IV. How many years do you have before you plan to retire?

_____

V.   List all the kinds of savings and investments you now have and the current balances.

	Investment Type	Amount
1.	_____	_____
2.	_____	_____
3.	_____	_____
4.	_____	_____
5.	_____	_____
6.	_____	_____
7.	_____	_____
	Total	_____

VI. Make an appointment with a banker or investment counselor and find out which kinds of investments are best for your age and financial goals.

COMMIT TO YOUR PLAN.

Therefore, my beloved brethren,

be ye steadfast, unmovable,

always abounding in the work of the Lord,

forasmuch as ye know that your labor

is not in vain in the Lord.

— I Corinthians 15:58

NOTES

A Faith Foundation to Financial Freedom

Commit to your plan.

Moving from caution to commitment may be risky. Do a self-analysis to see where you are; then determine where you would like to be. There are several critical areas to consider.

First is your relationship with God. Ask yourself what areas you would like to grow into. If we're just working in our purpose but not communing with God through prayer, we can block potential blessings. God seeks to have a relationship with us as we work in our purpose.

This year I committed to study the Bible more. As the head of the household, I decided that I had to become more grounded in God's word. To me, it was a great undertaking because I realized this new commitment—reading the Bible, praying, fasting—would affect my life and my family. But I reaffirmed the commitment of Joshua, "as for me and my house, we will serve the Lord." (Joshua 24:15)

Second, consider your purpose. Are you committed to stay with the purpose you know is right for you in life? Did you start down the right road and then turn back? Maybe you've gotten derailed along the way. We are each born for a purpose and that purpose should drive us daily. If your life is not in tune with your purpose, you are bound to feel frustrated and unfulfilled, making it hard to stick to a commitment.

Third is your commitment to family. Have you worked with the people closest to you to plan your future? Get your children involved; create positive saving and spending habits with them now so that their future will be financially secure.

Finally, self-discipline is probably one of the most difficult things to accomplish. What can you do differently to make sure you get different results? It's easy to talk, but remember only action is respected. Your integrity in following your plan is connected to every action, every day.

Set financial goals for your life.

Everyone has a purpose in life and your goals should line up with your purpose. Have some honest talks with people important to you and those who know you best—your closest friend, your parents, other family members and your spouse or significant other. Discuss with them what you want from life and how you envision the future. Involve them in your thinking. Talk to successful people you know and ask them how they set and accomplished their goals. Find a qualified person who is willing to be your mentor and advise you about your objectives and dreams.

Your financial goals depend on where you are in your life. If you are a single college student, your goals may be different from those of a single working parent the same age. If you are married, your goals may be different from those of someone newly divorced. Having health issues or children to put through college can affect your goals.

Your priorities change and you will have to balance and be flexible.

Home ownership is a key component to building wealth and is a goal I recommend. Within our society today, owning your home is the first step in your financial foundation walk.

Your current goal may be a new car, a bigger home, a nice vacation, the purchase of a retirement home or financial independence, whether you are young or retired. To some people, a "comfortable" lifestyle means a home in a nice neighborhood, expensive cars and private schools for the kids. To others, it's simply not having to live paycheck to paycheck and having a little extra money for movies and dinner out now and then.

MAKE ADJUSTMENTS AS TIME GOES BY.

Your priorities change and you will have to balance and be flexible. When I was 20, my goal was to be successful by the time I was 30. I accomplished that goal but setbacks caused me to start over. When I set a new goal, it was to get back to where I had been before misfortune hit me. I became a father pretty young and my primary goal was to always provide for my son and his education. One of my goals now is to be able to buy a condo in the Washington, D.C., area so I can be closer to my family on the East Coast and do more business there.

If you've built a good relationship with your banker, you'll have a partner to help you accomplish your financial goals as your needs change. Discuss your dreams and plans with your banker. Examine the resources you have and get your banker's advice about how to grow your savings and make investments that will help accomplish your goals with a good balance of risk and return.

If you've grown your passbook savings to $1,000, you may want to purchase a certificate of deposit (CD) that will earn a higher interest rate. CDs can help your money grow faster but, unlike passbook savings, they are not readily accessible without paying a penalty. You may purchase CDs at different terms—six months, 12 months, 24 months, for example. Generally, the longer you're willing to commit your money, the higher the rate.

BEGIN PLANNING FOR RETIREMENT NOW.

I asked a diverse group of people in one of my focus groups, "At what age should one start preparing for retirement?" The earliest response was 18 years; the latest, 45 years. The average was 22.7 years, which is a lot closer to the target than 45, I think! Twenty years, even with compounding interest, is probably not enough time to be fully ready for retirement.

Most financial advisors speculate that you must have about 75 percent of your average work income to sustain the same lifestyle in your retirement years. Not everyone expects to maintain the same lifestyle. Some want to simplify, but, then, others dream about traveling or enjoying other activities that may warrant more retirement income. How you want to spend your retirement will affect your retirement savings goals. Once you analyze what your spending habits will be in retirement and set some goals, visit with your banker or financial planner to see what products they offer to help you achieve your goals.

Goals mean nothing if you do not commit to them. You can allow some flexibility over time, but your commitment must not diminish over time. Commitment can turn dreams into reality.

Set Financial Goals for Your Life

I. List three short-term goals you'd like to accomplish in the next three years.

    1. _____

    2. _____

    3. _____

II. What is your most important long-term goal?

    _____

    _____

    _____

III. How do you envision spending your retirement?

    _____

    _____

    _____

IV. What is 75 percent of your average working income?

    _____

V. What steps do you need to take now to prepare for your long-term goals, including retirement?

    1. _____

    2. _____

    3. _____

    4. _____

    5. _____

A Faith Foundation to Financial Freedom

Connect to God.

Bring ye all the tithes into the storehouse,

that there may be meat in mine house,

and prove me now herewith,

saith the Lord of hosts,

if I will not open you the windows

of heaven, and pour you out a blessing,

that there shall not be room enough

to receive it.

— Malachi 3:10

NOTES

A Faith Foundation to Financial Freedom

Connect to God.

03 80

As believers, we must claim the promises in God's word. Scripture also endorses the tithe, the traditional tenth that is to be given to God through the established church. From beginning to end, the Old Testament talks of offerings to God and giving to God of our material possessions, because those possessions are ours only because God had blessed us with them. The tithe is first mentioned in Genesis 14, when Abram (later Abraham) gave tithes after a victory in battle to reclaim captured family. And in the final book of Malachi, the prophet is chastising God's people: "Will a man rob God? Yet ye have robbed me . . . in tithes and offerings." (Malachi 3:8)

But what follows is the promise of blessings, uncontainable blessings. Having a foundation of faith begins with believing God's word is true, and in acting accordingly. Stretched to the limit as it is? Afraid you won't be able to make ends meet if you give up that tithe? Where is your faith that God will bless you and take care of you?

Tithing is believing. Tithing is trusting. Like the old hymn put it, "His eye is on the sparrow, and I know He watches me." If you believe God's word, you have faith that He will take care of you with the 90 percent you have left after giving to His work.

If you believe God's word, you have faith that He will take care of you with the 90 percent you have left after giving to His work.

As John said in the second verse of his third epistle, may you prosper, as your soul prospers. Your soul prospers when you believe in His word and trust Him with the tenth. After all, it all belongs to God. He trusts you to take the 90 percent and use it well. Before you start talking about how you make that 90 percent work for you in this world, stop and pray about the 10 percent you should be giving back. That is the faith foundation from which you will begin to build your financial freedom.

The Bible does not shy away from financial issues. Money, riches, and worldly possessions are the gist of many of Christ's teachings, and He cautions about keeping riches in perspective. Three of the four gospels record the story of Christ's refusal to be embroiled in conflicts between God and the state when it came to money. "Render to Caesar the things that are Caesar's and to God the things that are

God's," are His words in Mark 12:17 (as well as in Matthew and Luke).

Connect with God through Bible study, prayer and fellowship with other believers and you will be blessed. Connect to God through returning His tenth to His work and you will be blessed even more.

Respect God's Tenth

I. Pray about the relationship between God and your money. Make the connection between your resources and your responsibilities.

II. If you currently tithe, explain when you first made the commitment, why you tithe and how you manage to keep your commitment. Share your story with your Sunday School class or with someone who may not tithe.

_____

_____

_____

_____

_____

III. If you are not currently tithing, what percentage of your income do you now give to support God's work?

_____

IV. List two ways you can find to set God's tenth apart from your spending.

1. _____

2. _____

V. If you do not tithe now, why not?

_____

_____

_____

VI. Do you think that 10 percent will make or break you? Do you believe that by not giving your tithe that you can do more with it than God can do with it?

_____

_____

A Faith Foundation to Financial Freedom

EXPECT POSITIVE RESULTS.

*These things have I written unto you
that believe on the name of the Son of God;
that ye may know that ye have eternal life,
and that ye may believe on the name
of the Son of God.
And this is the confidence
that we have in Him,
that if we ask anything according to His will
he heareth us;
And if we know that He hear us,
whatsoever we ask,
we know that we have the petitions
that we desired of Him.*

— I John 5:13

NOTES

A Faith Foundation to Financial Freedom

EXPECT POSITIVE RESULTS.

If we really walk in faith, things are never hopeless. We may make some sacrifices but if we petition God and truly give all things over to Him, we can trust all our needs will be taken care of because we are in God's hands.

For all of our investment in ourselves, we expect results. We work out so we are able to be healthy and strong; that's an investment in our physical well-being. The same applies to the investment in our minds. We educate our minds so that we are able to get good jobs, have better conversations, be more intellectually broadened in our horizons and enjoy more knowledge about subjects that interest us. We study God's word, pray and go to church seeking to be closer to God and find our true purpose. It takes a combination of all of these things—your mind, body and soul—to be all that you can be.

God is the author and the finisher of our faith. The expectation of each person is a measurement of our faith. If we have little expectation, that equals little faith. If we have great expectations, we have great faith. When we walk out on the waters of life, knowing Jesus is our savior, the first step of faith is a deep belief and commitment with all of our heart and mind, knowing that whatever we want, we can receive.

Ask God through prayer for the divine intervention that only He can give you. Then act as if it is already done. The expectation of its being complete is a move, an action. At that point, the spiritual realm and the natural realm have both been called upon. These are two principles of faith—prayer and action, expecting what God can do.

He is always there for his children. We are kings and queens of a heavenly realm watched over by our Father. He knows when you are in trouble. Think of it in this sense. If your child begins to cry, the first thing you will do as a parent is run to see what is wrong. The child feels, "Here is my parent, who cares what's happening to me." The parent's response is like God's intervention when we pray. He knows our needs and our feelings and He's there on our behalf. He never fails us. We can expect His presence to be with us in whatever we are going through.

Recently, a young stay-at-home mom with two children confided that she and her husband had begun to tithe. God had laid it on her heart during a Bible study. She is happy with the decision to tithe and feels blessed by God with so much more than material things. "We don't have enough money, but then we never had enough money before either. Now we still get by on a little less. I was able to help another church member who was truly in need and it was a blessing," she said.

You can expect good things to come from curbing your material appetites. Your appreciation of your own worth goes hand in hand with your attitude toward money. There is greatness in store for you if you align your purpose and your pocketbook and trust God to lead all facets of your life.

You can expect good things to come from curbing your material appetites.

God tells us not to lean unto our own understanding but to acknowledge him so he can direct us to know our future. So why wouldn't we trust him in all things? We need to connect to the source of all power, the true multiplier, the miracle worker. As the children of Israel fled the Egyptians, they had to cross the Red Sea—a seemingly impossible feat. Then Moses stretched forth the staff God gave him. The priest had to go first in the water before it became dry land, so the people could walk through it. This means we have to take action before God will lead us. Once we do, we can be confident of the positive end.

An optimistic outlook makes all the difference in your perspective. It may not happen overnight, but step by step, you can free yourself from debt and release yourself from the stress of financial difficulties. You have the power to choose to spend wisely, save prudently and give freely. You can focus and commit to your plan. If you're building on faith's foundation, you can expect positive results and God's blessings in your life.

FIND SOMETHING TO CELEBRATE

I. List the credit cards you intend to pay off first.

1. _____

2. _____

3. _____

II. What is your time frame goal for being rid of all credit card debt? Where do you expect to be financially by the end of 2005? 2007? 2010?

_____

_____

_____

III. Plan a little celebration as you pay off or cancel each credit card. Celebrate without spending more money!

SHARE THE REWARDS.

And let us not be weary in well doing;

for in due season we shall reap,

if we faint not.

As we have therefore opportunity,

let us do good unto all men,

especially unto them

who are of the household of faith.

— Galatians 6:9-10

NOTES

A Faith Foundation to Financial Freedom

SHARE THE REWARDS.

CROSO

Planning your spending and saving will help you find peace of mind that you'll miss if you are in debt and constantly struggling. Being able to give is rewarding even beyond that. I'm not in agreement with some who preach that if you give financially you'll be rewarded financially, too. In fact, I question that motivation. I believe giving is best if you expect nothing in return, but I can attest that there are rewards, at least spiritually and emotionally.

> *Giving is best if you expect nothing in return, but I can attest that there are rewards.*

Why give? Because you are thankful for what you have. Because you know how fortunate you are, even if you don't have as much as Bill Gates or Oprah Winfrey. Because sharing does as much for the giver as the receiver.

Distinguish good giving from unwise giving.

One of the big mistakes I've seen some people make is "carrying" others and allowing themselves to be used or duped into taking responsibility—often financial responsibility—for other people. Emotional money managers often fall into this pattern, a form of "codependency." It is not healthy. It reflects a lack of self esteem in the one who is doing the "carrying."

Supporting an adult child who refuses to work or providing money to someone who continues to do drugs is not the best kind of giving. It drains you emotionally, spiritually and physically as well as financially. Before lending or giving money to others, ask yourself, "Is this really helping?" A better solution—if they will accept it—is sharing your knowledge of money management and helping them find resources or plan a budget.

Personally, I think the United Way is generally a good way to give to the community. I've known a few people who resented feeling pressured to give to such campaigns, even though, of course, companies are not supposed to pressure anyone. Giving under pressure cannot compare to giving freely from the heart.

I've mentioned before a friend who taught his children to save 10 percent for short-term goals and 10 percent for long-term goals like college, give 10 percent to church and spend the rest of their money as they wish. This kind of teaching and discipline for children does not create resentment but helps establish a good habit of remembering to give something back.

BE WILLING TO SACRIFICE.

It's good if you can build giving into your budget, but some of the most spiritually rewarding giving requires sacrifice. If you'd like to be able to give more to your church or to a special charity, you can develop a giving strategy. Think creatively.

Look at what you spend on things you do for yourself and see how you might turn an expense into a gift. Take the money you spend on expensive coffee/espresso for a month and give it to a food bank. Commit your video rental money to buy books for a children's program at church or in the community. If you have things in good condition that are rarely used anymore, give them to a homeless shelter or church clothes closet. Encourage your kids to do the same with their toys.

Develop a strategy that includes giving as well as wise spending and saving, and get a sense of fulfillment that's unrivaled. Sharing the rewards of good money management is one of the best benefits of financial fitness.

Practice Wise Giving

I. List three ways that carrying someone is actually hurting them and blocking them from their life purpose.

    1. _____

    2. _____

    3. _____

II. List three ways that carrying someone is hurting or has hurt you in the past.

    1. _____

    2. _____

    3. _____

III. What can you do to prevent others from taking advantage of your generosity?

    1. _____

    2. _____

    3. _____

IV. If you had a windfall and could give generously to some person or cause, who or what cause would you want to support?

    _____

    _____

    _____

V. How can you help that person or cause with the resources you have now?

    _____

    _____

    _____

    _____

A Faith Foundation to Financial Freedom

SHOUT HALLELUJAH!

I will bless the Lord at all times:
His praise shall continually be in my mouth.
My soul shall make her boast in the Lord:
the humble shall hear thereof, and be glad.
O magnify the Lord with me,
and let us exalt his name together.
I sought the Lord, and He heard me,
and delivered me from all my fears.
— Psalms 34:1-5

NOTES

A Faith Foundation to Financial Freedom

SHOUT HALLELUJAH!

---- ✂ ----

I believe a plan is a dream with legs attached. So start by dreaming a bit. Consider what you value and what you want. Let yourself dream of the ideal situation.

Start writing. Put your dreams down on paper and begin to formulate steps that can help you accomplish them. You can't lead a rock band if you don't want to practice guitar, so whatever it is you're dreaming about, remember it won't walk in the door. You have to work and be prepared. Write down specific things you can do to get closer to accomplishing your dreams.

Begin now. It's always easy to put off changing a habit, like starting a diet after your birthday or cutting back on spending after the holidays. Seize the moment right now to start making adjustments to your lifestyle to help accomplish your goals.

Work your plan one day at a time. Alcoholics Anonymous uses this philosophy. Concentrate on the short term and before you know it, the days, weeks and months build up and your goals are being accomplished in the long term. Break your long-term goals down into smaller pieces. The old joke goes, "How do you eat an elephant?" The answer, simply: "One bite at a time."

Forgive yourself for past indiscretions and keep moving forward.

Put the past behind you. Well, that's silly advice, isn't it? The past *is* behind you! But the temptation to let the past invade the present and drag you down is a challenge. Forgive yourself for past indiscretions and keep moving forward. If you slipped last year, so what? You have a new plan now. If you slip today, get back on track tomorrow. As Dr. Martin Luther King, Jr., said, "Keep your eye on the prize!" Look to the future, not the past.

Share your plan with someone you trust. Talk about your goals with a parent, friend, loved one or trusted advisor. Be sure it's someone who will be a personal cheerleader, encouraging you continually and not focusing on setbacks.

You have those people who you respect and care for. I talked before about having a support system, your personal and financial dream team—the attorney you retain as counsel, a specialist such as a business attorney or tax attorney. When you start, make sure that whatever you're doing is on good, solid ground. That will at least give you a steady start instead of a shaky foundation.

Don't make excuses. Make well-informed decisions. Do your research about whatever goals and steps you develop. Understand what is required to accomplish your dreams and don't be fooled by "get-it-quick" solutions.

Be adaptable. Today's world is filled with change. If along the way, you need to adjust your goals because of things you can't control or have to be flexible with deadlines you set for yourself, don't let changes discourage you.

Praise God. Shout hallelujah. Seek God first and build your future on a foundation of faith.

Beloved,
I wish above all things
that thou mayest prosper
and be in health,
even as thy soul prospereth.
— III John 1:2